# BUT FIRST…

## A memoir
## of a backwards life

Heather Holloway McCash

Fire Flower Press

PUBLISHED BY FIRE FLOWER PRESS

ISBN-10: 0-9979869-0-5
ISBN-13: 978-0-9979869-0-7
First Edition

*For Vicki*
*Thanks for permission*

To Hannah,
Thanks so much for
being such a great part of
my family.

♡

Heather Holleman
xoxoxo

# TABLE OF CONTENTS

## POWERLESS

I am powerless
Without my pen
The words I cannot speak
Come to life on the page

The thoughts I think
Become one
With the ink
That I smear across the page

I am powerless
Without the empty space
To fill up
With my disgrace

My unspeakable acts
Become my lifeblood
As I slowly begin
To open up and share

## BUT FIRST...

My life began with drama, and it has continued ever since. I was born on March 22, and my place of birth was almost the hospital elevator. My mom's doctor was of course out of town when I decided to make my fashionably late entrance. The new doctor was worried about my position, so he ordered an X-ray. The X-ray showed that I was folded in half with my legs wrapped around my head, and I would be making my way into the world upside down and backwards.

My dad was in the elevator with my mom when she was on the gurney heading to the delivery room. They were stuck in the elevator because the doors kept opening and closing, preventing the elevator from going anywhere. My parents thought I was going to be delivered in there. Finally, the doors started working again. Once they made it to the delivery room, my mom found out she was not going to have an epidural, which was not the plan.

My mother has a lot of allergies like I do, and the staff was afraid she would have an allergic reaction to the epidural medication. They instead gave her gas to knock her out. She remembered the nurses telling her to push, and then I arrived—butt first, folded in half, and with my legs wrapped around my head.

I started my life a Frank breech and a huge pain in my mother's ass. This should have been her warning that life with me would not be easy.

One of my hips was dislocated during birth, and the doctors had to put it back. They put it back in slightly the wrong place, which would cause many problems later in my life. I have been doing things in a backwards way, in slightly the wrong place ever since.

## CHILD SIZE
### *Spring 2014*

On the last day of my thirty-second year, I finally came to terms with the fact that I am child-sized. During dinner that night with my friends, we had a let's-see-whose-hands-are-bigger moment just like in the cafeteria at elementary school. I found that my hands were still the smallest out of four other people. People tell me all the time that I am tiny. But I don't feel that way. I have been called a powerhouse. I have amazed people with my ability to get things done despite major obstacles. I feel strong and powerful. That does not translate into tiny in my mind. I realize I am petite; I can still fit into children's clothing. I don't want to wear children's clothing, of course, because I don't want to look like a kid. But no matter the price tag on my Calvin Klein suit, the style of my hair, or how much makeup I wear, I still look like I'm playing dress-up.

I have a tiny rocking chair that belonged to my mother in the fifties. It has a little music box on the bottom, and as you rock, it plays "Rock-a-bye Baby." The faster you rock, the faster it plays. As a child, I would sit for hours in the rocking chair, adjusting my speed to change the tempo of the music. I still have an affinity for rocking chairs to this day. When I got older, the music box broke. Then, about the time I turned fifteen, I couldn't fit in it anymore. I had developed hips and curves. I cried that day.

I went to San Francisco for the first time a few years ago. I got on the streetcar and started to put change in the change thing. Before I had paid the full amount, the driver said I could sit down. I was confused, but my jet-lagged brain did not have enough power to question him. I walked to a seat on the mostly empty bus. I looked out the window to watch the beautiful city unfold before me. The sun was shining to a degree of brightness it can only reach in California. I glanced around the bus, and my attention was drawn to the bus change thing again. I read the information on the sign. It said that the children's fare was seventy-five cents. This was the amount I had paid. I was twenty-nine at the time. This was not the first time I had been mistaken for a child, but it was the *only* time it had not pissed me off. The discount was fine with me.

I am aware of the benefits that can come with looking younger. I know they exist. People tell me all the time how great it is that I do not look my age. They tell me I should love that people think I am younger, and that one day I will— if I do not now. But as a person who has accomplished quite a lot in my now thirty-three years, I do not take it as a compliment when someone thinks I am twelve. I have a young face because I have, for the most part, taken care of myself. I have always been involved in some type of physical movement whether it was dance, running around and playing outside, Pilates, and/or walking all over Manhattan and Brooklyn. I also have food allergies, which have prevented me from consuming foods that can cause aging and other health issues. Looking young is also in my genes. I am a clone of my mother, and she looks much younger than she is.

Every few years in February, the age that people assume I am gets a little lower—or so it seems. When I was eighteen, people thought I was fifteen. At twenty-eight, people thought I was fourteen, at thirty, people thought I was twelve, and right before I turned thirty-three, someone thought I was eleven. I don't mind that I look younger than I am. I don't want to look old and haggard, especially since that is how my body feels sometimes. I do, however, have a problem with people thinking I am a child when it comes to my work or when people assume I have no experience or qualifications. This makes me feel like I constantly have to prove myself. I have been working most of my life. I am currently a Pilates Instructor. It took a lot of time and practice to become certified to teach Pilates. At times, I have been sitting behind the desk at work waiting to teach, and new clients assumed I was only qualified to "watch the purses." It just drives me insane when people look at me and assume that I have done nothing and am not old enough to even have a say in who is president of this country.

With all the struggles life has presented me in terms of health, career, and relationships, I have more life experience in my little finger than some people have in fifty years. Many people will never know what's behind this baby face. I have had four different careers in my thirty-three years. I've been an entertainer, a nanny, an office manager, and a Pilates Instructor. I have overcome a life-threatening illness. I have secretly brought down a few Wall Street titans. I have entertained some of our greatest entertainers. I have empowered and inspired people to be the best versions of themselves.

I still feel insulted when people think I am younger, but I can accept the fact that I am a small person. I do not have a small life, but I am small. People are always amazed by my life—by the ridiculous situations I have found myself in and how I have miraculously escaped. People look at me and see a naïve child but are so surprised when they look beneath the surface and see the wisdom and empathy that makes me who I really am. I have my blonde moments, but I actually have talent and insight, too. So let me surprise you. Let me entertain you with my stories. Come take a look into my compartmentalized boxes.

## PASSAGE OF TIME
### *Fall 2009*

I am always amazed by the passage of time. I may not pay attention, but it is still moving, changing, and sometimes remaining stagnant. It is too fast, too slow, or forgotten. I was walking one day in Manhattan, looking for a coffee shop where I could write. I walked for miles around the city, listening to jazz and remembering the many times I had been at the places I'd passed. I contemplated who had been with me, what season it was, what we had been doing, and what our lives had been like at the time. As I passed by one of my favorite casual restaurants, Dojo, I thought about all the friends I had eaten there with over the years. Some of them were no longer in my life. I remembered the situations we'd discussed over home fries and amazing carrot-ginger dressing—like the roommate drama we were having or how worried we were about getting a new job.

West Broadway was a street I often walked down from the very beginning of my time in New York. I remembered all the different stores and restaurants that lived there—the places that had survived and the storefronts that seemed cursed with their inability to keep a tenant. I thought about the friends who had walked those streets with me and the conversations we'd had about boys. So many times the conversation was the same but the friend was different. I was surprised to think about how important those situations seemed then, but they were no longer issues now. So many tiny details seemed like they would change my life back then, but ultimately they had no impact. Once I thought I had figured out who "the one" was for me. I even strolled through Bloomingdale's secretly thinking about what china I would register for. I dreamed about who would be in my bridal party. Not too long after that, it had all fallen apart.

How long ago it seems. I zoomed out of my time warp and landed in the present. Those situations that were so prevalent and all-consuming back then are either non-existent or over now… But they are worth remembering. It's important to take stock of what life has handed to me, what I have overcome, and what I've learned. I like to know how I got to where I am now.

## AUTUMN LEAVES
### *2013*

As the last summer breeze
Blew the first autumn leaves
From the trees
I felt your grip
Slowly start to slip
From my hand

You changed from hot
To cold
As the wind
Blew across my face

I thought it was not just a fling
There was more to it
But as the seasons changed
So did you

When I picked up the phone
I could tell from your tone
What you were going to say

Out of nowhere
The clouds burst around me
My heart shattered
My windshield covered in rain
The tears started down my face

I knew I was in trouble
When your kiss made me weak in the knees
Nothing good ever comes of losing control
Of losing your heart

The leaves have fallen
And now crumple beneath my feet
I learned my lesson
I won't change with the seasons
I'll stand tall and stay strong
Like an evergreen

## WELCOME TO THE ZOO
*Summer 2011*

I am a Pilates instructor. I also pet sit and housesit sometimes to be closer to work. I was warned ahead of time that the particular house I was sitting for had a lot of strange animals, but I was sure I could handle it. That assuredness crumbled when I arrived at the house to go over my responsibilities with the owner. The house was two-stories and on a hill in the middle of a country road. This was as far out into the wilderness as I had been in a long time.

The zookeeper—I mean homeowner—opened the door, and we awkwardly greeted each other. She launched right into the instructions and showed me around.

"Here are the dogs," she said. "They are both alpha dogs. They sometimes get after each other. The Corgi can go outside without a leash. The Yorkie needs to be on a leash, which is right here by the door." The grassy plant next to the door fluttered. "That's Scary Cat," she said turning toward the plant.

I noticed the eyes staring at me as he moved through the plant simultaneously hiding and trying to tear it up.

"Scary Cat is a hybrid cat," she continued. "He is still a kitten and is part tabby cat, part leopard."

"Oh really." I tried to keep my eyes from widening with fear. Oh man. I would be locking my bedroom door at night for sure.

"He likes to go in that plant because it is like the grass on the Sahara," she said with a laugh.

She moved through the house and led me up the stairs. "We lock the dogs up when we let the sheep and the goat out of their pen. But we will go outside later."

I typed into my notes on my phone as I wondered what kind of commotion happened to necessitate putting the animals that were *in* the house away.

"But sometimes we let the Corgi out with them. He likes herding."

As we made our way to the top floor, she pointed out the two cats lounging on the landing that I had not met yet.

"Here are the other cats, Fluffy and Skinny," she said. "They get along pretty well with the new cat but mostly they stay by themselves. Scary Cat likes to be with the people. He loves to snuggle." She turned around to continue the tour.

My eyes widened at the thought of Scary Cat cuddling up to me. "Well, okay." I said. This exotic, yet domesticated cat both intrigued and frightened me.

She shooed the cats away from the doorway of son number one's room. She shut the door behind us. "You have to keep the kids' doors shut so the cats do not get in and try to get the other animals."

I added that to my list. I did not want a massacre. Son number one had a chinchilla. "Pet him; he's really soft," she said.

I'd never pet a chinchilla before, and it was very soft although skittish. He hid in his tiny hammock inside the cage. She told me that they take dirt baths and that was the reason for the dust in the bottom of the cage.

We went to son number two's room. One of the cats was stalking around. She shooed it out, made sure there were no other animals in the room, and then shut the door. Then we went into the closet and shut that door. She knelt on the floor, and I joined her. There was a small cage with a tiny hamster inside.

"This is a robo hamster," she said. "They are the smallest and fastest breed of hamster."

I prayed that it did not escape. There would be no catching it and a very small chance it would survive the other animals. She gave me more instructions for my list, and I took a mental count of the creatures: two dogs, three cats, a chinchilla, and a robo hamster. Seven so far. After showing me all the specifics of the house, we went outside to see the sheep and the goat.

She pointed out which sheep was a male and which was a female and gave me instructions on how to feed them. They had a little barn, and the goat came bounding out when we walked up to the fence. She showed me how to tip the water trough over and where the hose was to refill it. She said she let them out once a day to graze and said they would come when you called them. I wondered how well that would work when I only had a few hours between classes in the middle of the day. I was having second thoughts as my list of instructions grew. I had spent way too much time living in New York City to turn around and live on Green Acres for a long weekend. I had to make sure all the animals were fed and that they did not run away or kill each other. I had made a commitment, though, so I had to do it. I pushed my fears of nature away. We walked back into the house and down the steps to check out the feed and hay for the livestock, which was naturally kept in the garage.

A few days later, I arrived at the house with keys and bags of clothes and food in hand. *I can do this,* I thought as I unlocked the door and made my way through to the barking dogs inside. The house was closer than my own house was to both of the Pilates studios I worked at. I would be able to avoid the normal back and forth of multiple rush-hour commutes and sometimes five hours of driving throughout the day. I set my stuff down in the guest room and closed the double doors so the animals couldn't do anything to my bags. Scary Cat quickly opened the doors, and I realized I would have to find a way to rig them shut since they did not lock. I made my way around the house, getting the lay of the land again and counting the pets. Once I was convinced everyone was accounted for, I headed out to feed the sheep and goat. I realized I shouldn't wear my tennis shoes in the pen since I wore those in the Pilates studio, but I had forgotten my rain boots I had planned to wear. So I put on my flip-flops instead. If they got ruined, I could easily replace them. I hadn't been in the pen for two minutes before the goat almost stamped on my foot with his hoof. I had to come up with a new footwear plan for the next day. A broken or injured foot meant no teaching, and no teaching meant no money.

I also realized I should probably not wear my workout clothes when dealing with the sheep and goat so I didn't smell like a farm animal when I arrived at work. I rifled through my clothes to find something that would be okay to wear while feeding the sheep and goat. I had nothing but workout clothes, a nice outfit, and a two-piece bathing suit. I decided the bathing suit would have to do. After a thorough search of my trunk, I realized I had nothing but flip-flops, high heels, and tennis shoes—no footwear worthy of a barn area. So I got creative. I put on my bathing suit and my tennis shoes, and then I put plastic Kroger bags over my shoes and tied them around my ankles so they wouldn't fall off. When I got back into the house, I left the Kroger bags next to the sliding door in the kitchen so I could use them again. It was a good thing the homeowners lived on a hill surrounded by trees. I looked like a crazy person feeding these crazy animals.

After feeding the sheep and the goat, I went to the bathroom to get ready for work before feeding the rest of the brood. I had been in the bathroom maybe two minutes when I heard a very loud, strange noise. I opened the door and did not see anything, so I started walking toward the sound. The sound kept moving. The house was circular, built around a large staircase. The sound went all around the house. Finally, I saw the source of the commotion run past me. It was Scary Cat. There was something on him, but I could not figure out what, so I ran after him as he ran into the kitchen and around again. After he passed me again, I realized he was wearing the

Kroger bags around his neck. I had no idea how I was going to get him to stop and get them off. He darted down the stairs to the basement. I only saw a flash run past me and heard the thump. I thought maybe I could finally get the bags off, so I walked quietly toward the basement and found the Kroger bags sans cat at the bottom of the stairs. I was thankful I did not have to corner the cat or worry about his accidental death due to Kroger bags.

I went back upstairs and put the dog food in two bowls. Scary Cat appeared behind me as I turned around to go into the bedroom before feeding the cats. I turned right back around because I heard yet another commotion. One of the dogs was barking, and a cat was hissing. I ran into the kitchen to discover Scary Cat had started to eat the dog food, and the Corgi decided he wanted to try and kill the cat. Thankfully Scary Cat was able to escape to the top of the dining room table while I screamed at the top of my lungs at the dog. This cat cost $5,000, and I did not have the money to replace it if one of the other animals murdered it. One by one, the other cats and dog cautiously made their way into the dining room. I could tell they were wondering if Scary Cat was dead. They all had an excited but curious look in their eyes. I checked the hyperventilating cat for bite marks, which thankfully there were none. I had never seen a hyperventilating cat and wondered, *do you give it a paper bag or just some space.* After a few minutes, the Corgi slowly tried to sneak into the dining room, visibly worried about his actions. I told him to go away. He padded out with a look on his face that said he knew how much trouble he was in.

My friend Monica and I were planning to go to the pool in the afternoon, but we were not feeling that motivated. We instead decided to enjoy the outdoors in our bathing suits. I needed to let the sheep and goat out anyway. I was scared to let them out of their pen, but at least Monica was there in case of disaster. I needed to clean out the water trough, which had to be done from inside the pen while the animals were out. So I opened the pen and out they came. I dumped out the water, and Monica sat on the deck laughing as she watched me move the hay around in my sexy outfit—a bathing suit, and tennis shoes covered with Kroger bags.

Once the trough had drained, I grabbed the hose and turned on the water. The hose was odd, but the zookeeper had shown me how to work it. I finally twisted things enough to get the water flowing into the trough.

I sat on the deck with Monica. The goat was the only animal allowed on the deck, and after a few minutes, he joined us. He loved carrots, so we fed them to him. We laughed as the goat hopped around the deck and the yard. It wasn't long before the two sheep decided they needed to join the party. But they were not allowed on the deck. I tried to shoo them off, but that did not work. Instead they pooped all over. This was a problem, but I figured I would just clean it up with the hose once the trough was full.

Finally, the water trough was filled, and Monica and I'd had our fill of animal and outdoor time. I grabbed the hose to clean up the deck. First, I had to remove the animals. Of course, the sheep did not want to leave the deck. I had no herding skills, but I finally got them off the deck and into the yard so I could start cleaning. By the way, sheep poop is a bitch to get off a deck. It got stuck in the little cracks in the wood, and it took me a good half hour to rinse. I tried to turn off the hose, but I couldn't. There was not a knob to turn it off at the house that I could find. That would be too easy. I had twisted one of the metal things to turn it on, but no amount of twisting would turn it off completely. I started to get frustrated, and then I looked up the hill. The sheep and goat were in the woods. I could not go in the woods because there were for sure ticks in there, and I could not afford to get Lyme Disease again. This was not going well.

Monica realized my frustration and offered to try to turn of the hose while I tried herding the sheep and goat again. I gave her the hose and started calling after the sheep and goat. They did not even turn their heads to look at me. They just continued eating the grass and then went farther into the woods as if to say, *bitch please.* Monica grew frustrated with the hose, so we switched. I worked on it again while she called after the naughty livestock. Neither of us had any luck. We switched again and again. Nothing was working. Monica sat on the deck, hot and tired. I sat down next to her, defeated. I had texted the homeowner to find out how to turn off the hose, but I hadn't heard back yet. I calculated the water bill in my head and added to that the cost of the two runaway sheep and a goat. I would have to pay for all of this stuff if I did not figure out a solution, and I did not have that much money. This weekend was proving to have expensive potential. We needed help. We sat still on the deck, letting the hose spray us both with a small stream of water. It taunted us and our cityness. We were too tired to move out of its way. I wished I could call my dad who was an animal guru and could probably fix the hose with one turn of the hand and get the livestock into their pen with one glance their way. But sadly, both he and Monica's husband, our only other possibility of help, were out of town. We were on our own with this one.

I finally had a light-bulb moment. I had two problems, but I could solve at least one of them with the other. If I couldn't turn the hose off, I would use it. I would herd the animals into the pen with the hose. Finally, I started to have some luck. I got the animals out of the woods and made Monica stand guard at the pen, gate in hand so she could shut it once we got them in. After a lot of running around, the female sheep went in first and her mate followed. The goat took a little more prompting, but Monica was right behind him. She shut the gate with a speed I'd never seen in our twenty years of friendship. During the sheep debacle, the homeowner finally texted me back. It was of no help. So we went back to our perch on the deck to sit and catch our breath. I had silently resigned myself to paying the water bill.

Suddenly Monica stood up. "I am winning," she said. "I am not going to let this hose win. I am winning."

I knew Monica was determined, but I'd never seen her like this. She turned her back to me, and I watched her arms move as she wrestled with the hose and the knobs as if it were a crocodile. Then the movement stopped. I did not hear the water spraying, and after a beat, she triumphantly raised her hand with the hose and turned around.

"I did it! I won!"

I inspected her work, and sure enough, she had turned off the hose. We cheered. We were done with nature for as long as we could possibly stay away from it. We headed inside to wash it all off and then went into the city to drink our farm life away.

## YARDSTICK
### *2009*

It was winter in New York, always dark and dreary. I was caught in the canyons of the midtown skyscrapers where the sun doesn't shine on gray days from November all the way to April. I walked for miles looking for an answer, looking for the light. I came across a Pilates studio only a few blocks from my office. As a teen I had been forced into Pilates at my professional ballet school. I fell in love with the method despite the constant shouts from our ballet teacher who had become a Pilates Instructor. She was trying to get us to do everything with our legs held parallel—the opposite of our ballet training in which we turn our legs out all the time. I don't know why, but this new type of movement spoke to me.

While I was in college, my father encouraged me to get my Pilates certification. He said it would be a good thing to have. I balked at the idea. I did not want to spend the money and had no interest in teaching. I did not have the time or money for classes, but I would do the exercises I could remember when I had the time. I eventually got a classical Pilates book, so I could do them correctly and in order. When I was sick with Lyme Disease and my achy joints hurt when I moved, I went back to Pilates and did as many exercises as I could—even though I couldn't do much—because I knew it was a healing practice. I'd had a stress fracture in my back and scoliosis as a teen, and Pilates always made me feel better. When doing six to eight hours of dancing six to seven days a week, there was potential for a lot of pain. Taking Pilates helped me to strengthen the muscles that dancing either over or underworked. The right side of the body often becomes stronger than the left for a lot of dancers, and Pilates exercises can help to strengthen those imbalances.

When I came to my darkest days, in those dark canyons on what were to be my de-stress lunchtime walks, I decided I should try out the Pilates studio near my office. I Googled the studio, and my ballet and Pilates Instructor from Nashville came up on its website. I found out later she was a teacher trainer. I knew if she was involved, I should be, too. I wanted to take a class but, every time I made plans for anything after work, I had to work late. So I stopped making plans and crept further into the solitude of my aching body. Then one bright spring day, work didn't work anymore. I could not stand one more day chained to my desk. I could not handle another day of hating my life. I had to find a career that did not make me miserable. I took note of the clearing in my mind. The sudden presence of the sun in the dark canyons of the city had revealed the answer to me. The next day, I handed in my resignation from my job and from New York.

I had a lot of time to think as I packed up my stuff from eight years of living in one apartment and over a decade in New York City. I needed a new phase in life. I thought about what I would do with my clean slate. I thought about what I would do if I had unlimited resources and time. I thought back to Pilates. My first instructor from Nashville, Sylvia, was the only person whom I would want to instruct me how to teach Pilates. She really knew her stuff. I decided to see what my hometown had to offer. When I moved back home to Nashville, I sought her out. The certification process would not be easy, but I could try, and I had nothing to lose.

When I moved back home, I was still having health problems. It was not as bad as it had been in the year leading up to my diagnosis with Lyme Disease and my subsequent thirteen-year battle, but things were still difficult. I had trouble speaking. I knew the words I wanted to speak, but they would not come out of my mouth. I had trouble writing. Communication, which had been my major in college and then my job, had become incredibly difficult. My muscles were in spasm most of the time. Sometimes it was a single muscle and other times it was a combination of several. I had almost constant muscle pain. I had been so flexible in my dancing days that my friends had called me Gumby, but now my achy joints did not want to stretch.

I found the Pilates studio once I was in Nashville. After getting over the initial nervousness, I went to my first class. I couldn't remember all the exercises, and it was a challenge to get my body to keep up with my brain. The class was a tower mat class, so there were leg and arm springs to deal with, which I had not used before. I had a hard time moving in general. I felt restricted by my joints and by my brain, which seemed to have trouble getting the messages to my muscles.

The more classes I attended, the more I remembered. The beginner mat training weekend arrived, and it was more of a challenge than I had anticipated. In a beginner mat class, Sylvia taught us all the exercises we would be learning to teach. We then had to go through the exercises one by one and teach each other the basics of the exercises using only our words. We were not allowed to demonstrate. We could not use our books. I had not taught anything formally before. The pressure to learn quickly and retain the knowledge made it harder for my brain to hold onto things. I wanted to do it perfectly right away. I had no patience with myself. Teaching something like movement is a challenge because the instructions, especially directional instructions, can be interpreted in so many ways. It was very rough. My mind had been a steel trap for so long. I rarely had to write things down to remember them. While in college, I could remember conversations I'd had in junior high, but now, when it came to Pilates, I couldn't remember that "Rolling Like a Ball" came before the "Series of Five." I felt like a failure. I felt like I had completely lost my mind. I kept messing up the words, saying them out of order, forgetting the transitions. We'd only had three days of training before our first test, and the pressure was getting to me. As a perfectionist, I hated to make one tiny mistake, but the exercises had become a soup in my brain. I did the best I could but still felt disappointed in myself, even though I passed.

I knew the real learning would begin when I started teaching. So the next week—after spending more time studying my book, practicing the words, and doing the movements myself—I had my first duet (teaching two people at once) in a friend's living room. I taught my friend and one of her employees early in the morning. We moved her coffee table out of the way, and I taught them the beginner mat class. Slowly, I started to make the connections to the exercises and to the corrections. I started to recognize the challenges of teaching someone Pilates for the first time. I studied the words and the cues. I said the words over and over while I commuted to my babysitting job. I taught friends over Skype. I taught my mom. I took classes so that I could improve my own technique. Finally, the words started to flow. The order came together. I didn't trip over so many words. I didn't have to think so hard about what came next.

I continued teaching and training. I completed certifications for Intermediate and Advanced mat and earned my certification to teach Xtend Barre. The more I taught, the more I improved. I began to get compliments on my teaching style. People really liked my classes, and I really loved teaching. I thought maybe this was what I should be doing with my life after all.

Teaching Pilates became my speech therapy, and after a while, I found that I could carry on a normal conversation outside of class. When I was sick with Lyme Disease, I had a hard time having conversations with people. It took me a lot of consideration to get the words out, and I could not speak as quickly as I had before. My words were often garbled because my brain wanted to work faster than my mouth, and the words just jumbled together. I started to get back to my normal New-Yorker time-is-money speech pace. I didn't have as much trouble finding the words, and the words had less trouble making their way from my brain to my mouth.

Learning to teach Pilates is not something that happens over night. I was often studying my training manual, trying to find more words to express the correct movement. I needed to learn how to look at a body doing the exercises and let it tell me what to say. I taught myself new cues to correct the movement every week. I instructed my body to move again by repeating the exercises. I strengthened my mind as I strengthened my muscles. The fractured connections between my brain and my muscles started to repair. The more I performed the exercises, the better I understood them. Having more understanding of how it felt to do the exercises correctly helped me to connect to the cues. Finding a connection to the cues helped me learn new ways to teach others how to overcome their own limitations and find the connection to the exercises in their bodies. The more I learned about the body, the more I understood about how Lyme Disease affected me and why.

The disease affected me for years before I received a diagnosis. When I began to make the connections about how sick I had been for so long, I felt robbed of my carefree youth. I spent so much time in my twenties depressed and exhausted, trapped in my apartment and my ailing body. I was unable to speak freely and unable to live to my fullest extent. Then I realized the tick bite had not robbed me. It had opened my eyes to the truth around me. It helped me see there was more to life than what New York had to offer. There was a life out there I was meant to lead, but I had to go through the suffering and fight the fight to fully appreciate what I have now—to know who I am and who I have to be.

After I took beginner mat training (a basic requirement), I had to wait more than a year for the comprehensive six-hundred-hour training course to begin. Once I was finished with the six-hundred-hour course, I would be a fully certified Pilates Instructor, and I could teach private sessions at Pilates studios. Most studios have a limited amount of group classes per day. Private sessions were a must to teach full time without another source of income. I was incredibly impatient for this process to begin. Once it started, I gave it my all. My top priority was Pilates, and I basically lived at the studio. I was there every day, observing, teaching, practicing, and training. I must have ended up with a thousand hours by the end. The stress I had experienced in beginner mat seemed like nothing compared to when I taught my first real client a private session at the studio while my instructor taught next to me.

My instructor, Sylvia, having known me since I was thirteen, knew how to push my buttons, and she did. Some days I was so mad at her for even walking into the studio. She drove me crazy with her high expectations. Sometimes if I did the slightest thing wrong, like sitting on the stairs during hour seven of observing and teaching, I would wish I had not even come into the studio because she was so mad at me. I was enough of a perfectionist myself, and her ability to know that the other apprentices and I were going to do something wrong before we even did it really added to the pressure. My fellow apprentices and I would often escape to the health food store behind the studio for coffee, food, and a bitch fest. We would complain about scheduling issues for tests and homework. We had to coordinate three to five people's schedules and work around the regular clients who were already scheduled in the studio. We had to navigate our practice times and teaching around the more experienced instructors, and we often aggravated them because we were in their way. We were not trying to get in their way, but we were usually limited on what we could teach, and that sometimes created issues of too many people and not enough equipment. We were all exhausted to varying degrees. We were trying to get all our hours in each week, but we were also working jobs on the side so we could afford the training. I went for months without a day off. Despite our high stress levels, we spent a lot of time laughing with each other.

Sometimes it was just pure giddiness. We might get frustrated with everything and each other, but at the end of the day, we were in it together.

I was rarely without my giant Pilates manual. The manual shows six hundred exercises broken down into beginner, intermediate, and advanced levels. In order to gain one's certification, a trainee has to know how to perform all of these exercises on eight different types of equipment. I was overwhelmed with the memorization that had to not only happen in my brain but also in my body. I had to learn the instructions for the set up and execution and the transition from one exercise to the next. I had to know what other exercises each exercise was similar to. Every exercise has modifications that a practitioner can perform instead of the traditional exercise if the person has an injury and cannot do the original exercise as intended. I had to know those variations and all the ways in which a person can advance from a variation to the next level. A trainee has to take four big tests, one for each level—beginner, intermediate, and advanced—and a final test at the end of the six hundred hours of training. The six hundred hours consisted of a mix observation, practice, self-practice, and teaching. We had to reach a certain amount of hours for each test before we could take it.

For some reason, out of the group of trainees, I was always tested first. I already had some classes I regularly taught that counted toward my hours, so the hours built up quickly. When I wasn't teaching, I held up the walls at the studio, garnering hours for observation.

Testing was always stressful. Each test consisted of a written and practical test, where we taught the specific level we had been working toward to a client or other instructor while Sylvia watched with eagle eyes. We lost points if we were late, if the client was late, if we went over or under the fifty-five minutes allowed, said specific words that were not allowed, did not say the name of an exercise, were not wearing shoes, or violated safety issues. When I tested, I prayed that Sylvia would be in a good mood and that the person I was teaching would show up on time. If she was in a bad mood, it usually affected the test results. I prayed that I would remember all the right things, say the right cues and not ever have a safety issue. My tests usually went well. That is until I got to the advanced test. Sylvia was in a bad mood, and my test body was experiencing back issues after the first few exercises. There was very little chance that I would pass, even if everything else went well. I could tell by the look in Sylvia's eyes that she had already made up her mind I would fail, but I had to keep going. The air was thick with her silent hostility. I knew my client was in pain, and I did not know what to do. One of the other instructors was teaching a client at the same time, and she could see the disaster that my test was turning out to be. She tried distracting Sylvia by asking her questions and engaging her in conversation, but it did not work. I wanted to stop, but I knew without asking that I could not do that. I felt completely discouraged. I had to go back and teach multiple exercises over and over. When my test body couldn't handle it anymore, Sylvia made me teach the air. It was terrible. I couldn't take it anymore but she kept going at me. Then she gave me terrible feedback. I felt like I had been doing it wrong all along, and I would never be good enough to finish. Sylvia decided I was her punching bag that day, and even though I promised myself I would not ever do it in front of her, I cried.

I was a miserable mess for a week afterward. I felt like a complete failure, even though I didn't do a terrible job. I almost gave up the training process, thinking that I could never be what Sylvia wanted me to be. Instead I persisted. I thought about when Gregory Hines had told a bunch of theater kids and me about going to an agent's office every single day without an appointment and waiting there all day until he finally got a job. I had to keep going.

Sylvia knew I could do better and was not going to let me be complacent. She told me that I needed to find more cues to help the client to advance the exercises. I went through just about every cue and every exercise, trying to find at least one advanced cue for each exercise. I didn't think I could work any harder at this, but I did. I taught every single person who could handle the advanced exercises. I decided I was going to prove Sylvia wrong.

When it came time for my re-test, I did prove her wrong. I completely kicked ass, and I became a much better teacher for all the hard work I'd put into it. It took me to another level of teaching. It pissed me off to realize it, but she was right. I did have it in me. I just had to work a lot harder to find it. I worked just as hard for my three final tests. I had to do the full advanced mat silently by myself while Sylvia watched. I had to take a written and oral exam. The part of the test that made me the most nervous was the practical exam. I had to teach a beginner client and an intermediate client at the same time. Most of the time, they were on different pieces of equipment and had different exercises to do. I had to tell each one of them what to do, how many reps to complete, give them cues to correct their form, give them hands-on assistance for difficult exercises—without missing a beat—and make sure they both had a good workout. Both clients had to finish their workout at the same time or within just a few minutes of each other even though they were not doing the same things. It made me sweat just thinking about it. The first time I practiced this test, it was a complete disaster. My intermediate person kept feeling left out, and my beginner client would not listen. But I found a couple subjects I knew who would pay attention and give me what I needed for the test. We practiced and practiced, making sure it was just right, and every time, it got better.

Finally, it was time for the practical exam, where I would teach the two levels at once. I made sure I scheduled it in the afternoon on a Saturday when no one else would be at the studio. I felt like I was doing okay, but I knew Sylvia would have something to say. She always had something to say. I was surprised that she remained silent the whole time. The clients finished their exercises at fifty-five minutes on the dot.

I looked nervously at Sylvia and tried to keep breathing. She took a breath and said words I don't think I had ever heard her say to anyone ever.

"It was perfect."

I asked her if she was joking, and she laughed. I ran to her and hugged her so tightly I almost knocked her over. This time I had tears of joy as she explained how far I had come, what a better teacher I was, and how hard I had worked.

I could not believe I was done. I had done it. After more than a year of waiting and nine months of training, I was a fully certified Pilates Instructor. I had set out to do something I never thought I'd wanted, in a place I'd never wanted to live again, and I'd found exactly what I was meant to do and exactly where I was supposed to be. Things were falling into place.

In order to maintain my certification, I have to take continuing education, eighteen credits every two years. I decided to go to New York so I could gain some new perspectives from other instructors and visit some friends. The Pilates studio near my office that I used to walk by all the time turned out to be the headquarters for the company I was certified through. I was doing my continuing education through that company, but the classes were being held at a different studio than the one I'd originally stumbled upon. As I was planning my trip, I did not see any time in my schedule that I would have available to go to the studio that had originally inspired me on my lunch breaks, the one that had reignited my interest in Pilates. I was a little sad that I would not get to try it out.

A few days before the training, I received an email saying the location had changed, and it would instead be at the headquarters on Lexington Avenue near my old office—the studio that had set me on this change in career paths. I was nervous as I walked once again through the canyons, this time in the pouring rain of December. I walked into the door of the studio and rode the elevator up. It was finally happening. As the weekend progressed, I realized how much

I had learned and changed over the past few years. I had come a long way since first yearning to practice at that studio. I had learned so much about my body and myself. I was able to use that knowledge to heal myself and to help others heal.

I finally had a break in the late afternoon the first day and decided to get lunch in my old work neighborhood. It had not changed much, but I certainly had. I was sitting at my favorite soup place looking out the window at busy Midtown East. I was kind of in my old patterns as if nothing had changed, but really it had. I envisioned a yardstick drawn on the corner of the kitchen wall with notches marked, showing how far I had come—how much I had grown. I realized I did not feel the same pressure, the same weighted-down feeling I usually had on my lunch breaks of those stressful years. I was free. Accomplished. I had finally found myself, and I was happy with what I had found. I had room for growth on the wall with the yardstick, but I had come pretty far from where I had been only three and a half years before.

# BROKEN TIRED RUSTY

Broken bobby pins
Elastic ends
Bits of lambs wool
Sequins

Crack in a mirror
Rusty metal barres
Rusty body
Rusty brain

Pieces of a life gone by
This tired body wants to pick them up
Put them back together
See what happens

Maybe I can do it
Maybe I can weave the frayed ends
Maybe life will change

Find the skinny mirror
Stand in the back
Watch what happens

Old friends
People who don't remember me at all
But I remember life in those halls

I want to feel the lift
Be the swing
Try the fouette
Lose myself in the turn

Open up the fractured pathways
From eyes to ears to brain
From brain to body
From heart to hands

Try to remember the translation
Of the words to the movement
Of the French to the English
Slowly coming back
Starting to feel

Becoming the leap
Feeling the beat
Letting the music
And the movement
Complete me

## BEEN THERE DONE THAT…
### *Summer 2011*

I was sitting outside the health food store killing time and getting ready to teach a barre class on a beautiful summer afternoon that wasn't too hot. I had just finished a late lunch and was contemplating the cookies I had bought when I heard someone talking behind me. Then I realized the person was talking to me. As a newly transplanted former New Yorker, I found this a little scary. I turned around, and there sat a cute guy with lots of tattoos and huge muscles, wearing a wife beater and Lululemon pants. Not so scary.

"Hey, what kind of cookie is that?" he asked.

"It's a vegan almond cookie," I said.

"That sounds really good. You've inspired me to try one this weekend."

"What do you do?" I asked.

"I'm a yoga instructor."

I laughed. "Well, I am a Pilates and barre instructor."

He asked me about my barre classes, and I asked him about his yoga classes. He said I should try one of his classes, and I made the case for him to take one of mine. Before I knew it, he gave me his number and said we should hang out sometime. I wondered if a yoga instructor and a Pilates instructor would be a match made in heaven.

He had given me his website information so I could look up his classes. The only classes I could go to were early in the morning. I am not an early morning exerciser and had never been to a yoga class, but I decided to try it anyway. I set my alarm and dragged myself out of bed. I questioned my decision to have coffee before class but took a travel mug with me anyway. I arrived at the class and someone else was teaching. I couldn't believe I had gotten up at five, and he was not there. I took the class even though I didn't know what I was doing. Maybe it was a good thing he wasn't there; he couldn't see me looking like an idiot. The next week I got up early again and set off for class. I was willing to give it another try. This time I felt much more confident in my decision to have coffee on the way. Again, another instructor taught the class, but I would not be deterred. A few weeks later, I tried one more time. The instructor did not show this time, so the class was canceled. I was not sure what to do, but I had not had time for coffee that morning, so I went to a cafe to wake up.

I decided to try a different approach. I sent him an email. I told him that I had tried to come to his classes, but that our paths hadn't crossed. I let him know that I still wanted to meet up with him. He asked me out on a date. I could not remember the last time I had been on a date. I spent a lot of time picking out just the right outfit and perfecting my hair and makeup. We went to dinner at a funky restaurant I had always wanted to try. He surprised me with his boldness and high energy. He was nothing like the Zen yoga instructors I knew. We talked about teaching and what we liked about it. We discussed the differences in the process to become a Pilates or yoga instructor. He told me about his former life as a chef in Miami and how he had recently bought a house. I told him about living in New York and my decision process to move back to Nashville. Then we went to a fun beer place downtown. He drove us there with his hand on my thigh the whole time. I was wearing my "red-equals-bed" peep-toe shoes, so I said yes when he asked me back to his place.

We had some wine and got to know each other a little better. And then a lot better. Red did equal bed. I stayed over. The next morning, he made coffee before I had to run to class. It was the best coffee I'd ever had! He spiced it with cardamom, which he said took the sting out of coffee. He wanted to have a lazy morning, but I needed to go take a Pilates class. I was about to step out the door when he said he had something for me. He dashed off to his home office. I wondered what was so important.

He returned carrying a shirt with his logo for his yoga classes on it. He said, "I only had sixty of these made, but I want you to have one." I was surprised. After one last tingly kiss goodbye, I was out the door.

As I changed into my workout clothes, I looked at the shirt sitting on the bed. Where would I wear it? I couldn't wear it to my Pilates studio. They would know what I had done. Why would I promote his classes when I could promote my own?

I decided the shirt should go away for a while into the bottom of the drawer along with the yoga instructor. He was trouble, and I had no time for trouble.

About six months later, I was running through the health food store on a short break between classes and training. I was about to go to the checkout when I stopped dead in my tracks. There was a girl wearing *the shirt!* I grabbed my phone, put it on the camera setting, and tired to nonchalantly chase her around the store until I got the picture. I wondered if he was a clichéd, skirt-chasing, yoga instructor and if he gave a shirt to all his flings. Is it his mark? Is that how he lets everyone know he's had his way with the lady in the shirt? Then I realized I had been there, done that, and gotten the T-shirt. I shook my head at my discovery. I guess she had been there, done that, and gotten the T-shirt, too.

## CLOSE BUT NO BARBRA
*Summer 2010*

Time to go. New York was not so new to me after having lived there for more than a decade. I wanted out. I started looking for jobs. I wasn't sure what I wanted to do, but I knew I had to be in Los Angeles. I could go the safe route and get a desk job, but I did not want a desk job like I currently had. I was working at a PR company in Manhattan and had no desire to work with a bunch of frat boys who had moved their frat house—complete with a mini-keg—from Connecticut to an office building in Midtown East.

I thought that a non-profit might be a better environment for me. I found some interesting options and fired off some résumés and cover letters before going out of town for a family reunion. Right before I left, things at my job got really tense, and for the first time in my life, I did not want to go back to New York. I had applied to the one place I thought might actually work, but that weekend I was looking back over my résumé, and realized it had a huge, glaring mistake on it. They were never going to call me. I was completely frustrated with myself, but there was nothing I could do.

After a much-needed relaxing weekend, I had to go to Atlanta for my flight back to New York. I was trying to fight back the tears as I walked my dog outside the airport. That's when I saw the only other lone shoe I had seen outside of New York or Los Angeles. It was my sign that I was on the right track. Everything would be okay. I got back to New York without incident. The next day I received an email from the company I thought would never take me. They wanted to do a phone interview. My mood changed as my luck shifted. LA felt like more of a possibility than ever before.

I did not know much about what the company did, so I Googled right away and almost had a heart attack at the results. I was aware the firm handled charitable and political giving for some celebrities. I was not aware the person most well known for working with this firm was none other than my favorite person in the whole world, Barbra Streisand. Not only had the owner of the firm and Barbra been working together for a long time but they were also best friends! I let out a scream and quickly covered my mouth. This couldn't be true. Google had to be broken. There was no mention of Barbra in the job description I'd initially found, but now it was right there on the internet in black and white with pictures to prove it. I continued my research with shaking hands. I wanted to tell everyone I knew that I had a job interview with a firm that worked very closely with Barbra, but I did not want to jinx it. I could not tell anyone for fear of fate getting in my way again.

The next day, I dialed the Los Angeles number for my interview with the woman whose job was up for grabs. It went very well, and I could not believe what she told me. She had been to Barbra Streisand's house! And her job required her to talk to Barbra on the phone all the time! It would be a lot of work and learning, but oh what I would give to work with Barbra Streisand. I felt good about the interview. This could actually happen. It was all I could do not to call my mom and tell her the good news—along with everyone else I had ever met.

The next interview with the vice president went so well that they wanted me to fly out to Los Angeles to meet the owner. This time I had to tell my mom. She was very excited, and I made her promise she could not tell anyone, not even my dad, what the interview was for.

My trip to LA could not come fast enough. When I finally arrived, I spent the weekend looking at apartments, eating all the vegan food I could fit in my stomach, hanging out at the beach, and seeing friends. I found ways to distract myself from the excitement Monday had to bring. I found a great apartment in Santa Monica—my favorite place in the world—that was a mile from the office and three from the beach. It was just too perfect. I found a shoe every day. Finding lone shoes was my sign I was on the right path. Then Monday came, and I spent the whole day getting ready for the interview. I could barely eat I was so nervous. It was finally time to go. I left early to give myself plenty of time to get there and spent half an hour sweating while waiting in the car on the verge of hyperventilation. I finally decided it was too hot in the car and not too early to go in. I put myself back together and went into the office. My hands were cold, sweaty, and shaky. My sometimes-twitchy muscles were jumping, too. I tried to breathe to calm myself so I could make the best first impression.

After what felt like an eternity, they took me into the boss's office. She would be in shortly. I sat on the couch looking around. The office was filled with pictures of Barbra posing with politicians and other celebrities. I realized that Barbra had probably sat on this very sofa. Before I could freak out, the heads of the business walked in. They were very friendly, although the president was intimidating. They asked me a lot of questions about my work experience. Then they asked me a question about Barbra.

The president said, "If Barbra Streisand called and wanted to talk to you about Wall Street reform, could you do that?"

I blurted out, "Of course I can. I would love to talk to her about Wall Street reform. I definitely think Wall Street needs some changes."

I was trying to be eloquent and smart in my answer, but all the while I was thinking that if Barbra Streisand called *me*, and I realized it was *her*, I would immediately *die*, so I would not be able to talk to her about anything. But if I was able to survive the shock, I would absolutely talk to her about Wall Street. I wanted to tell them that if Barbra Streisand called and wanted to talk to me about how the world was flat, I would say, "Why yes it is, Barbra. Isn't it sad that we've been wrong all these years?" I refrained from my humor and did my best to explain to them that I was on Barbra's side without telling them how much I loved her. At one point they mentioned that the job would require doing some writing for her. This was probably the hardest moment for me not to lose control. I once again tried to explain to them, without sounding creepy, that I could handle that. Overall, the interview went well. I wasn't too shaky, and I don't think I appeared to be too nervous.

Before I boarded my return flight the next day, I received a call. The HR person said the company loved me and wanted references and a timeline of when I could be out there if I got the job. I knew this was going to work. It had to. Besides, I found a shoe every day except the day I'd had the interview. I was so excited; I could have flown myself back to New York.

I waited anxiously for my call back. This had to happen. As much of a bitch as fate had been to me, she could not be so evil as to dangle this particular carrot in front of my face without letting me have it. It was not like I was looking for a job with Barbra. The opportunity had fallen into my lap. And things like this did not just happen halfway.

One week of waiting turned into three. My chances had looked so good. I needed and wanted this so bad. I found a shoe on my lunch break and got excited again. I got a call when I got back to work. I knew who it was. I could tell by her tone that the HR person did not have good news. They had absolutely loved me, she said, but they'd found someone who already lived in LA and worked in the non-profit sector. It would be an easier transition for her. I said that I understood, and she told me I should let them know when I made it out to LA because they might have something for me in the future. I wanted to say that I would be a better candidate—that I wanted it more than anyone could ever want anything—but instead, I thanked her and told her I'd get in touch down the road.

Even after all the rejection from my career in entertainment, I had never been so heartbroken about not getting a job. I could not believe I had been so close. So, so close to my absolute hero.

So close, but no Barbra.

## DRUNK AND DRUNKER
### *Spring 2008*

In early May, I was attending a benefit for a Spanish dance company with a Cinco de Mayo theme. I was all decked out in a gorgeous dress that looked like it was made for me. I had bought it with part of my government stimulus money. *Thank you, Uncle Sam!* I was supposed to meet a friend, but she wasn't feeling well. I wanted to meet a reporter from CNBC, who would be there, and I wanted to network and meet some new people, but I did not want to do it myself. I asked a few other friends, but no one could go. I called a friend, Cable Guy; he lived near the club where the benefit was being held. I asked if he wanted to join me. Unfortunately, he couldn't because he was having people over for drinks at his place that night. He had started a very successful cable network and had an amazing townhouse. He told me to come by after the benefit, and I said I would.

I arrived at the club where the benefit was being held. I didn't know anyone, but I knew I would be fine once the dancing began because I was never alone for long once I started moving. I drank a margarita while I was working up the nerve to start a conversation. I tried not to drink too fast, but I was nervous and didn't have anyone to talk to. One drink turned into two. I found someone to talk to for a few minutes and then another person. Finally, the dancing began. I danced with my conversation partner for a while. Eventually we needed to catch our breaths, so we hit the bar and ordered margaritas.

I was getting tipsy after three drinks in just two hours. The tipsier I became, the feistier I became. About twenty minutes before the benefit ended, I found a guy sitting by himself. I asked him to dance. He was a little shy, but I told him not to be. Shy Guy and I danced and talked. I was having a good time. He asked me for my number, so I gave him my card—one of many I'd handed out, thanks to my tequila-fueled courage.

Once the benefit was over, I drunkenly teetered over the cobblestones in my super high heels to my friend's place. It's a wonder I didn't fall on my face. I told myself I wouldn't stay long. It was a weeknight, after all. I really wanted to see my friend, whom I hadn't seen in months, and then go home.

The townhouse was about five stories, and with all the music and loud conversation, no one heard the doorbell. I should have taken that as a sign that I needed to go home, but I would not be deterred. I waited a little while and then rang it again a few times until someone finally buzzed me in. I walked up four flights of stairs to the floor the party was on. I tried to find Cable Guy, but he was nowhere to be found. I was talking to some very nice people, and they offered me a drink. I said, "No thanks, I can't drink any more tonight."

But a little while later, I decided to have some wine. I didn't think that could do much damage. I kept looking for my friend, but every time I found him, he disappeared into the crowd. My feet were aching, so I sat down at a table and talked to a guy whom I really didn't want to talk to. I gave him my card anyway because it was networking night. I wanted to meet some new people, and I really wanted a new job. The alcohol was diluting my sense of discernment. I was handing my card out willy-nilly.

Someone came by with a couple of drinks and offered me one. I took it. It was really good, so I drank it quickly, and when he came by again half an hour later, I grabbed another one from his hand. Needless to say I was flat out drunk by this time. The next thing I knew, the old guy I had been talking to began making out with me. I didn't want to make out with him, but in my tipsy state I wasn't sure how to make him stop. Finally, I pulled away and went outside for some fresh air.

While I was outside, another older guy, Photog, started talking to me. He was nice, and we were having a good conversation. He was a photographer, and we talked about photography stuff. I couldn't remember why, but I left him and went back into the party. I had my camera out and was taking lots of pictures. I asked a friend to take a picture of me in my hot dress since I didn't have one yet—and it *was* a hot dress. I decided in my sloshy state to do as many poses as possible. Unfortunately, my friend dropped my camera on the floor. I picked it up to survey the damage. The retractable lens was stuck out and it wouldn't go back in. I was devastated. I never go anywhere without my camera. This sobered me up a little bit, and I remembered I still hadn't talked to Cable Guy.

I finally found him, and we started having a conversation. After we had been talking for a while, I realized that everyone had left, and it was just the two of us. We were both leaning up against the wall in the kitchen chatting. His kitchen was being used for the set of a major network TV show I had been watching. I was leaning up against some TV kid's artwork on the wall and looking up into the professional lighting that hung from the ceiling. The next thing I knew, he was making out with me. I couldn't believe it. I really didn't think I was his type, and he was about forty years older than me. I knew I had to stop. I was way too drunk, and I didn't want to get taken advantage of by an older man for the second time that evening on the set of a prime time show. Somehow I got control of myself and told him I needed to go home. I looked for my coat, but it was gone. Someone had stolen the coat I had just bought the day before. It had the perfect 1960s-style Peter Pan collar and three-quarter-inch sleeves. It hit me perfectly at the waist. It was sturdily made (for an H&M coat) and was a steal at $60. I had no idea someone would turn around and *steal* it from me. I was incredibly upset. My friend gave me one of his coats and walked me down three flights of stairs to get a cab.

I got in the cab and was thankful it wasn't a long ride. It didn't really matter, though. I leaned over and started puking on the floorboards. The cab driver grumbled and cursed, but I just held up the $20 I had in my hand over the partition while I continued to puke. Once I stopped, I told him to pull over and let me out. I was almost home and only had to walk around the roundabout to my apartment complex. The cab driver was happy to get rid of me. I hobbled a few steps to a lamppost, put my hand on it to steady myself, and then puked again. Finally, I walked the block to my apartment.

The next morning, Friday, I woke up at 10:30. I was supposed to be at work two hours prior. *Oh god.* I threw on a robe and ran to brush my teeth and wash my face quickly. I was washing my face when the doorbell rang. *What now?* There were ten people outside of my apartment. They needed to check a leak. I was so pissed off. "You are going to have to come back in half an hour!" I slammed the door and quickly threw on some clothes. I didn't even know what time I had gotten home the night before. I obviously hadn't set my alarm.

I ran downstairs and out into the pouring rain. *Great.* I got in a cab and called work to tell them I had overslept and was on my way. After I hung up the phone, I realized that they were taking me out to lunch that day for a belated Administrative Professionals Day gift. Because I was "such a great find" and "so good at what I did."

I finally arrived at work after twenty minutes in rainy traffic. The news anchor on the television at my desk was wearing a neon green shirt, and I had to look away. I was still a little drunk and the colors were making me sick. We were leaving for lunch soon. I really didn't want to sit close to anyone for an hour, and the last thing I wanted to do was eat.

I survived lunch and the teasing from my co-workers and even began to feel a little bit better. I checked my email later and saw that I had a message from Shy Guy. He asked me out. I was so embarrassed! I decided to just ignore it. Then twenty minutes later, I received another email; this time it was from Photog. "I was kissing your lips, and then you disappeared into the night …" *Oh my God!* I had made out with two older guys!

My leg started itching, so I rolled up my pants to see why. I had a huge gash on my knee. I hadn't noticed it in my rush to get out the door that morning. The memory returned from the drunken recesses of my mind. I had been walking out of Cable Guy's house when I'd tripped and fallen flat on my face, thanks to the tequila and the four-inch heels. I guess I'd scraped up my knee in the process. I was horrified that I had been such a mess.

It was not a productive day—thanks to my horrendous hangover—but I managed to get some work done. I was worried about the state of my dress, my shoes, and my camera. The dress was a limited edition, so I couldn't replace it, and I had spent too much money on the shoes and my camera to replace them anytime soon. I finally escaped the office and ran to the camera shop across the street. There was nothing they could do to fix it. They said I would have to send it off to the manufacturer, but it would be cheaper and worth it to just buy a new one. I didn't know what to do. I couldn't afford to buy a new camera. I'd only had that one for six months. But I was never without my camera, so this was a problem. I didn't know what I would do if I found a shoe and I could not capture it with my lens.

I raced home after the bad news, almost sick again about what might have happened to my brand new amazing dress and equally amazing shoes. I looked around, but I didn't see them anywhere. I went to my closet. Somehow, even though I was extremely inebriated, I had managed to hang up my dress, put my shoes back in their box, and put my purse in its little protective bag. I hadn't puked on anything. *Whew.* I was relieved it was all over and went to my bed to pass out. Even though my clothes—aside from my coat—had made it through the evening unscathed, that crazy night would haunt me for an untold amount of time.

Sunday afternoon I got another email from Shy Guy telling me that I had helped him to overcome his shyness and I shouldn't be the one who was shy now. I still ignored him. I was completely embarrassed by my drunken behavior.

Six months later, I was at Cable Guy's home again for a party. I brought along a friend for protection and made sure I didn't drink too much. I was talking to some friends, and I saw a guy I remembered from the night of debauchery. We struck up a conversation. He said that he had tried to email me afterwards, but I never got back to him. "Oh you did? I don't remember that." Then it all came rushing back. I had mistaken his email as being from another older guy. I had drunkenly made out with *three* older men that night, not just two! I was caught off guard as the realization set in. I did not know what to say, but he stood there waiting for an answer. I prayed my friend would come and save me as some weak excuses tumbled out of my mouth.

"Oh wait, I remember your email," I said. "I am so terrible at emailing people back. I am so sorry I forgot to respond. I have been so busy lately." I knew there was no other way to dig myself out of that hole. "I have to go find my friend now."

I found my friend and dragged her to the fifth floor bathroom.

"Leah! You are not going to believe what else happened the night of my drunken escapades."

"What else could have happened?"

"Well you know how I made out with two guys over forty that night?"

"Yeah," she said through her giggles.

"I was just talking to this photographer that I remember from that night. What I did not remember until just now was that I made out with him, too. So that brings the total to three men over forty that I made out with in one evening."

Leah was laughing her ass off when I noticed a lacy pair of panties on the sink. I pointed them out, and we both cracked up. Clearly I was not the only one who liked to have a little too much fun.

A few hours later, and after having a good time, we left the party unmolested.

## TICKED OFF
### *Summer 2006*

I started working on Wall Street in PR in 2006. I knew it would be stressful but I did not realize that Wall Street sucked the soul out of its employees. I had no idea there would be lasting effects in my life and my body. After about six months of it, I developed an eye twitch. I was frustrated that part of my body could move on its own without my control. Sometimes just my left lid would flutter a bit, and other times, I felt the twitch near the outer corner of my eye.

At first, I assumed it was simply the high amount of stress manifesting itself in my body. Then one day I noticed the twitching in my thigh muscles. I would be sitting still at my desk and suddenly my thigh would just start jumping or sometimes I could just feel a subtle twitch deep in the muscle. Then my calf muscles began to do the same thing. Then the tip of my nose, cheeks, and fingers. Before I knew it, the twitching was everywhere, and it hurt. At any moment, any muscle or combination of muscles could just start moving. I had a hard time sitting still, and as a former dancer who once had so much control over my muscles and my body, I found it maddening to not be in control.

I got a new job, thinking a change would help. Maybe if I quit working on Wall Street I wouldn't have so much stress. The new job was fine at first, but the stress levels continued to rise, and my health continued to decline. I went to see my doctor to find out if anything else was going on. He thought I might have MS (Multiple Sclerosis), so he sent me to a neurologist.

The neurologist tested my reflexes and watched me walk around his office. He asked me to stand with my eyes closed, and then he tried to push me over, but he had no luck. He asked me to lift one leg, and then he tried to push me over again. I passed the balance test with flying colors. Of course, that was no surprise to me. As a dancer I had to perform complicated choreography and turns while balancing on one leg on pointe. I practiced balance relentlessly inside and outside of my ballet classes. Then when I moved to New York at eighteen, I continued to practice balance on the crowded subway each time it lurched into or out of a station. The neurologist ordered an MRI to see what was happening in my brain.

When the tech told me to lie on the scanner and remain completely still, I had a hard time not laughing at her. I was getting an MRI because I could not be still no matter how hard I tried. Even though I had adjusted to small New York spaces, I still had claustrophobia sometimes. This was one of those times. First, my head went into the pristine white machine, and then my whole body followed. The loud rhythmic banging scared me. I tried to stay calm, knowing that stress would only make me tremble more and that the more movement I made the longer it would take the tech to get the right images. I was in the machine for an anxiety-inducing hour. After I got out, the tech showed me the multicolored pictures of my brain.

I sat for an eternity in the waiting room to see the neurologist for my test results. The MRI results suggested that nothing was wrong with me. He told me I did not have MS; everything was normal. I was relieved not to have MS, but I knew things were not normal. Something had to be wrong. I was not looking for an earth-shattering diagnosis, but I also knew my body and myself. Sure, I could walk in a straight line, and my pupils had followed his finger when he'd waved it in front of my face, but something wasn't right.

I let my general practitioner know what the neurologist

had said and went on with my life. I did not know what else to do. My health slowly got worse. I started to forget things. My boss would ask me to do something simple like change a dinner reservation by half an hour, and I would completely forget. I thought maybe it was my overload at work. It was not easy to keep all of the things I was responsible for straight all the time. But it kept happening. I started double booking myself. I almost walked out of the house without shoes one day. I knew I needed to find a solution to the problem. I carried a giant notebook and wrote down everything my boss said—anything I had to do and anything I needed to remember. Throughout the day, I would check the list to make sure I had completed everything. It was helpful, but my brain, which had once been so sharp, now seemed like a sieve.

Then I started dropping things. At first just a pen or paper. Then I dropped heavier things like my keychain, books, my phone, my Blackberry. I could barely hold onto anything. I dropped things all the time or accidently threw things at people if I was trying to hand them something. It was maddening. If I dropped something on the floor, sometimes it would take me three tries to pick it up again. My depth perception was way off, too. I had bruises everywhere because I kept running into my desk, my bookcase, even doorframes.

I was very depressed. I had been depressed before, but this was different. I felt like my life was falling apart. I hated my job. I had a terrible roommate. I thought those were normal things to be depressed about. But I knew that my depression went deeper. No matter how hard I tried I could not be happy.

Little stabbing pains deep in my muscles would catch me off guard. Sometimes the pain was quick; other times it would last for hours. Any part of my body could be in pain at any given time, but most often my legs ached. Muscle spasms and muscle twitches came along with the pain. One night I was sitting on the couch watching TV. I had my hands resting in my lap, and my ring finger on my right hand started jumping and twisting to the side slightly.

My body was constantly moving. I could never sit still, and it drove me crazy. I just wanted to relax. I thought once again that maybe stress was the problem, so I tried as many stress-relieving activities as I could. If I was getting stressed out at work and I could get away from my desk for lunch, I would walk with a purpose to the East River to get away from the noise of busy midtown. On one of my walks, I found a beautiful waterfall built into a building. There was a nice garden and plenty of tables were I could eat lunch or write. The sound of the flowing water and the fact that I was doing something for myself helped eased the tension. I thought maybe I needed to exercise more. Maybe if my muscles were tired, they would stop jumping around. I started walking on the treadmill at a gym near my house. Then I tried running. It did not help. It only added to the exhaustion and pain.

I had a hard time hiding the twitching and spasms. I was so terrified of people knowing there was something wrong with me. At times I would have to excuse myself from my boss's office for a minute—even though he was speaking to me—because I didn't want him to see that my entire thigh muscle was moving by itself.

Soon, it seemed, I had no control over my body. My knees would give out. This was something that had happened in the past, so it did not scare me too bad at first. Then one day I got up from sitting at my desk and my legs wouldn't move. I fell to the floor because I had nothing to hold me up. Luckily no one was around to see me.

I stopped going to parties because I was too tired. I didn't want to hang out with my friends because my face wouldn't be still, and I didn't want them to know something was wrong with me. I had trouble with my vision, and after twenty-eight years with perfect vision, I had to get glasses to see things that were far away.

I was really scared. I felt like I was falling apart and

couldn't find any answers as to why. I did not think it was normal for a healthy twenty-something to be falling down and forgetting things. I was always in pain. I knew something was wrong. I didn't want anyone at work to know I was sick, but I had to go back to the doctor. I had a hard time leaving work in the middle of the day because I had a ton of responsibility. The people in the office did not like it when I was away from my desk, and I had been in and out of the doctor's office a lot the past few months with one thing after another. I knew my boss would grow suspicious if I said I had another appointment. The neurologist made me wait for a long time the last time I was there. I tried to get an appointment early before work or after, but he did not have any appointments available. I had to see him, so I had to take an appointment on my lunch hour. I didn't want to tell my boss that I had to go back to the doctor when I had just been there twice the week before. The neurologist said if I came at noon, he would see me right away so I could get back to work.

I was still really worried about going to the doctor. I got to his office and sat down. I waited for fifteen minutes. He came out of his office, got his mail, and went back in. I waited another twenty minutes. He came out with some of the mail he didn't need. Then he went back into his office. I couldn't wait any longer to see him or I would be late to work. I told the receptionist that I had to leave and left in tears. I had really hoped I would be at least somewhat closer to finding out what was going on with me. But instead I didn't have any answers, and my health problems were scaring me. I obviously couldn't trust this neurologist to help me if he was going to read his mail while I was supposed to be having an appointment.

I decided I needed another opinion. I needed answers. I was so angry with this doctor for wasting my time when something was seriously wrong. It may not be a big deal to him, but I knew whatever the issue, it was only getting worse without treatment, and I couldn't get treatment until I had a diagnosis. I found a neurologist close to my office. This one was much more compassionate. I was so tense about the whole process of trying to find a diagnosis, dealing with doctors, and hiding everything from my co-workers. I was so stressed and scared once the doctor finally came in that I cried in his office for half an hour as he asked me questions about my symptoms. He was much more patient and caring. He listened when I talked to him, and he was as helpful as he could be. He suggested therapy and prescribed Valium. He said he needed to do an Electromyogram that would test my muscles with electric shocks to see if they responded. I said I'd try anything.

The Valium only made me more exhausted. The Electromyogram was horrendous. They stuck needles in me and shocked my muscles with electricity to see if they would respond. The doctor said that I needed to do the test on a Friday because it would take a lot out of me and I would need time to recover. The test didn't show anything wrong. I asked the doctor why my muscles were jumping all around so much that I couldn't sit still and why my legs would give out from underneath me. How can nothing be wrong? He once again suggested a specific type of therapy, Neuro-linguistic Programing. I told him I had done therapy and didn't feel I needed it anymore. I was completely frustrated and stressed out. I knew something was wrong with me. I just needed someone to tell me what that was. I was in diagnostic limbo. I had exhausted all of my resources in terms of finding answers, so I gave up looking. I once again went back to living my life to the best of my ability.

I had been getting craniosacral massages for about a year, and that seemed to help. I had less brain fog. My muscles still had a mind of their own, but they didn't hurt as much all the time. I went to California for five days for a much-needed vacation. I decided I had to move there and vowed to begin the job search as soon as I returned. Unfortunately, I got vasculitis from the plane ride home. Vasculitis is a rash from blood vessels bursting and rising to the surface. It can leave itchy, red dots on the skin that scar. I'd had it once before, and my doctor said that if I ever got it again, I had to come back for more tests because it is usually a symptom of Lyme Disease. I had been tested for Lyme Disease a few times before but always had negative results. I went to my general practitioner, and he ordered more tests. The nurse practitioner, who was also trying to figure out what was wrong with me, encouraged the doctor to order another Lyme test.

A few days later, I was standing on the corner of 14$^{th}$ Street and 5$^{th}$ Avenue when the nurse practitioner called with the results that I had tested positive for Lyme Disease. The nurse practitioner listed the things I couldn't eat, the antibiotics I would need, and described the severity of the disease. I would no longer be able to move to California. She explained that if I wasn't better in three months, I would have to see a specialist, which would cost me a minimum of $800 for one visit. She talked about the possibility of PICC lines, IVs, and monthly—maybe even weekly—specialist visits that insurance would not cover. I had no idea how I was going to handle all of this information. Some people who have Lyme Disease have to stop working. Some people have died from it. Some people never recover from their symptoms.

I finally promised the nurse I would get my prescription and keep her updated. I walked down the street to my massage therapist's office and sat in the waiting room trying to process all the information. I couldn't even remember getting a tick bite. I didn't realize until a couple months later—when I still wasn't better after two months of antibiotics—that a tick had bitten me when I was fifteen. I'd had a lot of illnesses as a teenager and young adult. They were all probably related to the Lyme Disease. Because I was so active and mostly healthy, I was able to fight off the disease. Now, with all the stress from working in corporate America, my body was no longer able to win the battle.

I had heard of Lyme Disease, but I thought it was rare. The day I had been bitten, I had been hanging out at a friend's house. I remember the gloomy, gray spring Sunday afternoon. I walked outside onto her deck for two minutes to look at her backyard. There was a large field behind it. I leaned my hips against the wood of the deck, turned around, and walked back inside. The next day I was at one of my dance studios getting dressed in the bathroom. I just happened to glance at my hip and saw a tick on it. I screamed. I was so terrified. I knew ticks were bad news. I knew I had to get it off me as soon as possible. Not knowing the correct way to remove it, I just yanked it out. I'd left the head stuck in. I did not know I needed to go to the doctor or get antibiotics. The bite itched, but I just put hydrogen peroxide on it. I probably had the telltale bull's-eye rash, but I did not know that was a sign of infection with Lyme.

Looking back, I realized that the weight I'd gained out of nowhere when I was fifteen was not a result of hitting puberty. Despite dance classes and endless rehearsals (about four to eight hours of exercise a day), I had gained weight, and I didn't like my body. Some of my muscles seemed to disappear over time instead of being built up. When I was sixteen I had been walking to class at a summer intensive ballet workshop. I noticed that my left calf muscle that had been strong and healthy before had become one with my leg. My calf muscle no longer had any contour; it had almost completely disappeared. Additionally, I would get sick with two or three things at once. During tech week for *The Nutcracker* with Nashville Ballet when I was fifteen, I had a sinus infection, bronchitis, and the flu. Getting sick with multiple illnesses at once became a trend; I was sick much of my last few years of high school.

On the first day of what was supposed to be my last semester of college, I got really sick. I went to the doctor and discovered I had a 104-degree fever. I was so sick I was hallucinating. I was planning on going to school after I went to the doctor, but he told me to get my medicine from the pharmacy and go straight home. I called my mom to tell her I was sick, and I sounded so awful that she got on the next flight. She stayed with me for a week. I couldn't sit up for more than twenty minutes at a time. I had never been so sick in my entire life. I got well enough to live my life again, but I never felt like I fully recovered from that illness. I couldn't figure out what was wrong. That spring, I was so tired all the time. It took all the energy I had to take a shower and get ready for the day. Sometimes I had to lie down after getting dressed. Then I would fall asleep and often even miss class. I knew something was wrong, but I was not sure what. After a while I got my energy back. I thought maybe it was my allergies causing the fatigue. I had no idea Lyme Disease was rearing its ugly head.

After I finally remembered the tick bite, I called my general practitioner to tell him. He suggested I make an appointment with a specialist, since it sometimes took months to get one. I took the first available appointment, which was about two months away. My mom flew up to New York to go with me. I somehow found out about a special screening of the documentary about Lyme Disease, *Under Our Skin*, at the International Film Center the day before the appointment. We decided to go to get a better idea of what we were dealing with. Watching the movie was helpful—to see that other people were going through some of the same things I was. I was heartbroken to see how deeply affected the people they interviewed were. There is a section of the film where they ask people how much money they have spent on Lyme Disease in the past year. The scene is a montage of people giving figures from the tens of thousands to hundreds of thousands of dollars for one year of treatment. At one point, there is a little boy who starts to cry as he says that he just wants to be normal. I started to cry too while watching because I felt exactly the same way. I just wanted to be normal. I just wanted to be a normal twenty-eight year old who could be happy and live freely, but I felt trapped by my debilitating illness.

The first specialist appointment was overwhelming. They had warned me I could be there all day, so I took the whole day off from work. One doctor and a nurse practitioner ran the clinic. They had so many patients in their office that they divided them between the doctor and the NP, based on how sick each patient was. I was sick but not sick enough to see the doctor. I saw the nurse practitioner for the examination and initial discussion of symptoms, treatment, and what to expect. I was in his office for about two hours. I was very thankful my mom was there to take notes. My brain was not strong enough to remember everything. He took my vital signs, tested my reflexes, and checked my body for swelling. He explained all the different types of tests I would have to take and the different options for antibiotics. If the oral antibiotics did not start to work soon, I would have to take them intravenously, and that could cost about $2,000 a day. I prayed I did not have to do that. There was no way I could pay $2,000 a day minimum for antibiotics alone. Before he sent me to the nurse to get blood work, he said I was the healthiest, sickest person whom he had ever seen. He gave us a folder of information that contained pamphlets regarding tests I needed to take outside of the office. It also held a two-page list of the medicine, vitamins, and supplements I would need.

I walked through the lobby to the IV room to get my blood drawn. My blood would be sent all over the country for three different Lyme tests in three different states to verify that I did have it. Lyme Disease is a spirochete, a corkscrew-looking thing that can hide in your organs. A lot of times people get a false negative when they are tested for Lyme Disease because it does not show up even though they have it. That makes the testing process tricky. Specialists send blood samples to different labs that specifically do Lyme testing, so they have multiple tests that can be compared and verified. I also had to have my vitamin, hormone, and endocrine levels checked, because Lyme wreaks havoc on the immune and endocrine systems. Lyme soaks up all the good things in the body and breaks down its natural defenses. Many Lyme patients are so sick and malnourished from having the disease for so long that their bodies cannot absorb vitamins and antibiotics orally to heal; they have to get them intravenously or through a PICC line.

The IV room was an interesting place. A little light seeped through the windows that looked out onto the brick wall of the next building over. The glow mimicked the tiny bit of hope we patients had for ourselves. The long ivy plants looked like they needed some care. The walls of the room were lined with recliners that each had a wooden platform armrest for patients receiving an IV drip. The magazines were piled up like in any doctor's office, but they remained untouched.

I sat down in a chair next to a rolling cart of vials and needles. I glanced around as the nurse filled out my seventeen vials with my information. "This is a lot of blood we need," she said. "Do you want to come back another day and just do half today?" I did not want to come back another day. I was overwhelmed with the possible issues a serious illness could cause. But despite how scared I was about my health, I was even more worried about my job. I was trying to keep my illness a secret from my boss and co-workers. I knew they did not like me, and I did not want my illness to be an excuse for them to fire me. I already didn't know how I was going to pay for all of this with a job. If I lost my job, I would not be able to afford treatment. I had to ration my time out of the office. "I think I can do it. Let's just see how many we can get." She began with the first vial, and I turned my head.

"Do you not like needles?" she asked.

I shook my head no as I concentrated on thinking about something else.

"Well, let's just get this done as quickly as we can so we can do something more fun like talk about the bill," she said with a laugh. I laughed too.

Even though she saw sadness and illness on a daily basis, she had a great attitude. I looked around the room at the people there. I felt like I was intruding. A few people slept, others talked. One man read a book. Family members sat quietly nearby in support. The situation looked desperate. Some patients looked so sick and beaten down by the disease that they had given up hope. This was just part of their routine. They just showed up and did what they had to do before going back home and going to bed.

I was so sad for them, but I was also worried about myself. I didn't want to be in one of those chairs hooked up to an IV. Seventeen vials of blood would determine whether or not I would have to take up regular residence in one of the recliners. The blood would help decide if I would receive my antibiotics in pill form, PICC line, or IV. Most people who had been sick as long as I had been were receiving antibiotics through PICC lines. I was so afraid of that. The nurse filled vial number ten with blood and checked to see if I was okay enough to endure seven more. I told her to keep going. Once we made it to the last few I started to feel lightheaded, but I persevered. I sat in the chair for a little while.

When it was time to go, I went to the counter to get more instructions, set up another appointment, and pay. Most Lyme specialists do not accept insurance because it is a very political disease, and the consequences of doing so include a lot of court dates, the possibility of getting shut down, and more trouble than it's worth. The lady at the front desk told me how to submit my claims to insurance but that I would probably have to do it multiple times and that the chances were slim that I would get reimbursed. I took a deep breath and paid her $1500 for my first visit. I wondered how I would be able to keep this up.

Lyme Disease is a political disease because treatment is long and costly. Insurance companies do not want to pay for it, and as a result, patients end up having to pay out of pocket for most of their treatments. Many patients don't have the money to pay. Often doctor's offices and hospitals get stuck with the bill or patients cannot receive treatment. Lyme Disease is also very hard to diagnose because the disease hides in the organs. Most doctors do not know much about Lyme Disease, and some do not believe it even exists. One of my friends who also had a lot of trouble getting a diagnosis for all of her strange medical problems was finally diagnosed with Lyme Disease, as well. Her doctors did not want to diagnose her, even though all signs pointed towards Lyme. After finally receiving treatment, my friend asked her nurse why she had such trouble getting a diagnosis. She said that if she had cancer or AIDS, she was certain she wouldn't have gotten so much pushback. Her nurse told her that if she had cancer or AIDS, she would be dead in a year or two, but because she had Lyme Disease, they could still be treating her when she was eighty.

Much of the treatment for Lyme Disease is controversial, as well. Lyme takes everything out of the body, breaking it down from the inside out. The body, trying to fight back, has to use all its resources. This often leaves the body depleted of vitamins, minerals, and hormones.

Taking medication and supplements isn't enough to treat Lyme. I had to change my diet. Aside from my sweet tooth, I eat pretty healthy. I try to only eat unrefined sugar—and because of my allergies—I eat mostly vegan with the exception of fish and chicken. I cannot eat any dairy at all because I am highly allergic, and it makes me extremely ill. I already ate a very restricted diet, and I was not excited that I had to restrict it even more. Lyme can cause weight gain, and because of that and the way Lyme feeds off of certain foods, I had to severely limit myself. All of my favorite vegetables like peppers, potatoes, carrots, and eggplant were off limits because they cause joint pain and swelling, and I already had plenty of that. I couldn't have spicy food or food that had been fermented. I couldn't eat starches or fruit or have alcohol because these things could cause excess yeast in the body, and Lyme feeds off of yeast. I was supposed to eat low-glycemic foods and avoid dairy—not a problem. I had to cook everything I ate—or better yet, steam it—in order to avoid getting an infection from raw food. I already knew a lot about food and was very conscious about what I ate. There was a time when I had a list of food allergies a mile long and I had to cook 99 percent of my food from scratch. My new diagnosis would now require more research and more trial and error in regards to my diet.

I needed to find new ways of cooking and eating that would both nourish and sate me. The problem was that it took me a long time to make the food. I spent about four hours in the kitchen every night trying to make dinner for myself from scratch. My multiple lists of restrictions often canceled each other out until I was left with just plain vegetables and grains. All of my favorite things were things I shouldn't eat. I couldn't eat carrots because of their glycemic number. I couldn't eat pasta or bread for the same reason and because they caused excess yeast. I couldn't have tamari or balsamic vinegar because they were fermented. I tried to make some salad dressing with olive oil and fresh herbs so I could have some flavor in my life. I put it in the fridge, and the next day it had solidified. I didn't realize you couldn't just put olive oil in the fridge. I started making a lot of stuff on my George Foreman grill, but the grill was small, and items still took forever to cook. To complicate things, I was so tired that everything I did took me ten times longer than it should have. I had a lot of trouble with my motor skills, so there were plenty of nights that I cooked for two to four hours, picked up the plate with the food, and dropped it halfway between the three feet from the kitchen to the table. Then I would just call my mom and cry. My poor dog knew I was so upset he didn't even rush over to eat what had fallen to the floor until I told him it was okay.

My Lyme tests came back positive. I did have it. The other tests showed that the Lyme had severely depleted the vitamins and minerals in my body because my immune system was using everything to fight the disease. I had to take more vitamins and supplements to help my body build its defenses back up and replace what it was using to keep fighting the Lyme.

My doctor decided to keep me on the less-expensive oral form of antibiotics, rather than getting antibiotics through a very expensive PICC line. Getting antibiotics from a PICC line would require daily IVs, a lot of work, and more expensive medications. I was very sick, and there was a lot of speculation that I would need a PICC line. I had no idea how I would take care of it all and pay for it on top of that. I was relieved that I did not have to deal with that and could just continue taking oral antibiotics. The specialist planned to increase my dosage steadily over the summer. This meant I would need to come in for periodic blood work to make sure my liver was not affected. I also could not go out in the sun because I could get severely burned from the amount of Doxycycline I was taking. Doxycycline increases sensitivity to light. As a pale person who gets a sunburn by just thinking about going outside, this was not exciting news.

During the summer, Manhattan turns into an oven, thanks to the sun's heat bouncing off the pavement, the exhaust from cabs, and the emissions from skyscraper air-conditioning units. Plus, the subway becomes a sauna. I had at least a mile walk to and from the subway every day and lots of walking in between that. I was going to have to stay completely covered and wear sunblock. I had a feeling it was going to be a long, hot summer. I bought a floppy hat that I wore almost every day and found a few light-weight, long-sleeve shirts. None of my clothes fit me anyway, since I couldn't eat anything but vegetables and grains.

One day I was walking in my quiet neighborhood. I stepped off the curb, jaywalking to get to the World Financial Center walkway, and before my foot could hit the pavement, I fainted and fell in the street near the curb. Thankfully it was a Sunday, and there were no cars around. I regained consciousness quickly. Thankfully I did not hit my head too hard or hurt myself too badly when I fell. But it did scare me. I was starting to get scared that I would not be able to take care of myself. I worried that I would have to move home and let my parents take care of me. I wondered if it was safe to be out walking alone. I needed so much energy just to walk to the subway in the mornings. I considered getting a Zip Car membership for the days I had to do a lot of walking, but I did not trust myself to drive. I couldn't afford it anyway.

I went to a rooftop pool party in August when I was taking my highest dose of antibiotics. I had not been in a bathing suit all summer, and I just wanted to be normal and have fun. We were mostly in the shade, and I had on a ton of sunblock, but there was a short period where I did not wear my cover up. I went to the bathroom to wash my hands, and the cold water felt like someone was digging ice picks into my skin. I thought maybe I was just too hot, but it got worse. My skin was not red, but my hands and arms were burned for sure. I could not even stand in the cold section of the grocery store without feeling cold shooting pains in my hands and arms for weeks.

Antibiotics were not the only medication I had to take. I also had to take anti-malaria medication. I had to take cod liver oil right out of the bottle. It was so gross I would gag every time, and it's a wonder it stayed down.

At the end of August, I went to see the specialist. I took the day off from work so I could go to the doctor and then spend some time with friends who were visiting from out of town. I thought my appointment would only take an hour or maybe two at the most. But the next thing I knew, I was being sent to the IV room.

I had gone in for a checkup and had to stay for the next six hours to get an IV of iron since my latest test results had shown that my body could not absorb that vital nutrient. My eyes widened when they stuck the needle in. The blood went up through the tube and back in as the clear liquid began its journey. I tried to relax but it hurt, and the slightest movement of my arm resulted in more blood and pain.

I looked around me. Some people were sleeping. A few people were talking about their symptoms and their journeys. There was no cell service to save me from these painful conversations. I felt some of the same pains they were discussing. I had some helpful ideas to add, but I did not feel like I should interject. I listened and kept my thoughts to myself. I heard bits of my story in theirs. I realized we were all out there in the world fighting our singular battles on our own crusades, but we were all in combat with the same demon. I wanted to speak up. I wanted to be a part of the conversation. Instead I reveled in my silence, knowing we were all in it together.

I had a busy weekend coming up. About thirty of my friends were coming into town from all over the country for a girls' weekend. They were all part of a group I had come to know through Marilu Henner's website. We all made a point of getting together with Marilu every few years. I was also teaching an online class for Marilu over the weekend that would allow those who couldn't attend the get together the opportunity to participate from afar. I was looking forward to seeing my friends, some of whom I had not seen in about eight years. The iron IV saved the weekend. I had been so tired I wasn't sure how I would make it through all the excitement. But the iron gave me the strength I needed and gave me back enough of my old self to have a fantastic time.

Taking shots is another necessary evil of Lyme Disease treatment. My Vitamin D and B-12 levels were often so low that I had to get shots or give them to myself. I was not a fan of needles, and even after years of having weekly to bi-weekly allergy shots, I could not look when I was getting a shot. Now the doctor wanted me to do it to myself. I could have gone in to the clinic to have the nurse do it, but there were times when I had to get the shots every day, and that would mean missing more work. Plus, a clinic visit meant forking over more money.

I resigned to do them on my own. I went to the doctor late one afternoon, and the nurse told me what to do and then supervised while I gave myself a shot. I was so scared to have to pierce my own flesh with the needle, but the nurse was waiting. So I sucked it up, stabbed myself, and pulled the plunger. It didn't kill me. I was still alive and breathing, albeit a little shaken up. The next day, while on my own, however, I could not bring myself to do it. I sat there for twenty minutes staring at the needle and then my bare flesh. I tried counting to three. Too scared. I tried deep breathing. Still too scared. I finally decided that the part I feared the most was stabbing in the needle. But I had to give myself the shot. That was not going to change. So instead of stabbing, I just pushed it in slowly. It hurt a lot worse, but I wasn't as scared to do it.

I had to work sixty- to seventy-hour weeks to get through my ridiculous workload. I also needed to work overtime to help pay for my medical bills. I couldn't pay my rent myself most months or buy food, but I could just about make all those medical bills go away. Thankfully, I had my parents to help me financially when my medical bills were depleting my bank account. I hated needing their help but I had no other choice.

Over Christmas break while home in Nashville for the holidays, I met up with my friend Jill. She had studied at the Kushi Institute where she learned about macrobiotics. I had tried everything over the past nine months in terms of food. She gave me some very valuable information about Lyme Disease and macrobiotics that I believe saved my life. I did not follow macrobiotics to a T, but I did as much as I could, and it made a huge difference. The most helpful thing was Umeboshi plums, a traditional Japanese food. They are pickled plums and you can get them at Asian stores or health food stores. I could, at the very least, have a pinch of one every day or so. They taste really salty and it takes a while to get used to them, but they put your body back in balance. They make your body more alkaline, and when your blood is alkaline, disease can't live in it. I finally started making real progress with this change in my diet. A few months later, I got my periodic Lyme test, and it was gone!

The nurse practitioner was very pleased with my progress. Not many people get Lyme out of their system so quickly, and I'd only had a year of treatment. There is the possibility of it coming back, but at least it was no longer active. I slowly started to decrease the antibiotics, supplements, and vitamins. My body started to take care of itself without all the extra help. I hadn't exercised—other than walking—for a year, so I was thrilled to get the green light to start doing so again. I knew I couldn't do a lot at first, and I would need motivation. I decided to get a Wii and a Wii Fit. It did wonders for my hand-eye coordination, and it helped me get back into a routine.

Spring had finally arrived, and my eyes were opened as if I had been asleep for the past fifteen years. I was a new person. After being so sick for so long I became more aware of myself. I realized I did not like my life anymore. I did not want to work in PR, I had grown tired of New York, and I finally realized what I wanted out of life. I wanted to live. I wanted to be happy. I did not want to just work all the time and have no life like I had for most of my life. I found myself on a path that I did not recognize, working non-stop in the corporate world after a lifetime of working in and studying the arts. It was time to change my path and get back to my roots.

## DOG HOUSE
*Summer 2005*

In New York in 2005, I got an assistant job so that I could be creative on the side. I thought it would be a nine-to-five job—unlike the twelve- to fourteen-hour days I'd been putting in babysitting. I thought I would have time to myself on nights and weekends. I thought I could get health insurance. Boy was I wrong. It was my first full-time office job. I was a permanent temp at the Epitome of Corporate America. They'd hired me to keep up with their busy phone lines in their public relations department. I was excited to have a job that was kind of in my field of communications. I didn't know much about the finance industry, but I saw the job as an opportunity to learn more.

There was not enough money in the executive office of the headquarters of Epitome of Corporate America to hire me as a permanent employee. But there was enough money to give the top executives tens of millions of dollars in bonuses every year. Still, there was not enough money for me to have health insurance or a paid day off every now and then, even though permanent employees got about a month off. I was at the bottom of the totem pole, but a few months later, the company recognized that I had more to offer and promoted me to executive assistant. However, I was still a permanent temp. I loved my job, though. I thought I could work toward becoming a permanent hire because I knew I was valuable beyond my assistant title. That did not happen, thanks to my extremely bitchy boss who not only made my life miserable but also stood in my way.

I had two vice presidents to handle, one of whom was the problematic bitchy boss, Three-headed Dog. When it was announced at our weekly meeting that I was assigned to the Three-headed Dog, my friend in the group looked at me and tried to say he was sorry with his eyes. He knew my days were numbered with this change. Three-headed Dog was notorious for micromanaging, acting like a total bitch, and for kicking people out of her revolving door. She tried her hardest to make my life miserable, but I resisted. She micromanaged everything, even phone messages sent to the entire team that had nothing to do with her. If I did not pick up her phone on the first ring, I was in trouble. No matter how detail-oriented my projects for her were, they were never good enough. Her negative attitude spread like toxic fumes as she entered the office each of the few days a week she worked. I was an assistant to several people. It was hard to please everyone at once, and generally she was the one who was unhappy. I was not responsible for a lot of projects related to her work, so not much I did should have upset her. She did have a problem with me doing things for my other executive whom I liked to call Former Mormon. His workload was much heavier than hers, and he was studying for a serious work-related test, so at times, he needed more help than others. Three-headed Dog basically wanted me to sit and wait for her to summon me. Other people in the department said I made the office a much nicer place with my smiles, jokes, and good work ethic. They were happy to have me. But Three Headed Dog usually wanted to bite my head off.

The Epitome of Corporate America was a cutthroat place for its female employees. Three-headed Dog didn't like that I was going places, and her put downs got to me. I started to feel the pressure that I had, for the most part, previously brushed aside. She got pregnant right after I started working with her, and her hormones made everything even worse. There were days that were unbearable, but I decided her jealousy was not going to get in my way. I had wanted an office job so I could be creative on the side. The long hours, stress, and berating started to affect my creative time. Having to be responsible for Three-headed Dog and all her ridiculous drama and micromanagement made me rethink sticking around. Thankfully she went on maternity leave.

After Three-headed Dog was out of my hair, the office was a different place. And I was not the only person who was happier about the change. Everyone was more at ease. I only had one executive to be responsible for, so I was assigned some special projects. I took on even more responsibility and started working on projects that were usually reserved for vice presidents. I worked without supervision for the most part and made decisions that directly affected the reputation of the company. I worked with heads of businesses on photo shoots for major publications. That was probably my favorite role. It got me out of the office and away from the negativity. I worked with photographers and met new people who were very high up in the company. I blossomed that summer like the buds on the trees.

The bitch came back at the end of summer. She only worked four days a week, but it was four days too many. She did not like that I had my own projects. She was threatened by the big boss's recognition of my talents and abilities. Her level of micromanagement rose quickly. She berated and yelled at me for no reason in front of the entire floor of employees. She made me meet with her and the Former Mormon twice a day. They would go through the checklist of stuff they wanted me to complete. I resented this because it wasn't protocol for assistants to have these meetings, which only served to take up valuable time. She was a terror to anyone who dared get in her way. The stress she put on me started showing up in my body. It began with an eye twitch. It moved to my eyebrow, to my cheek, nose, and eventually all over. Any part of my body could twitch at any moment. It wasn't noticeable to others unless I pointed it out, but it concerned me. I made a doctor's appointment to get the symptoms checked out.

Former Mormon started causing his own trouble. The building had a cafeteria on the basement level. Once Three-headed Dog had returned from maternity leave, he made me go to the cafeteria and get his breakfast. His orders came complete with a list of instructions. He demanded that I put brown sugar in the bottom of the cup, add a layer of oatmeal, then a layer of brown sugar, then another layer of oatmeal, and repeat the process until the cup was full. Then I had to put raisins on top. The coffee had to have just the right amount of skim milk plus three packages of Splenda. The cafeteria was always crowded in the morning. I had to wait in line usually to get to each thing I needed. The cafeteria employees gave me dirty looks as I went back and forth to the brown sugar and the oatmeal. The line to pay was also long. Sometimes it took about twenty minutes to go through the whole ordeal. Former Mormon usually got to work early, and Three-headed Dog did not like it if I was not at my desk the second she arrived. I wasn't required to get breakfast for Former Mormon every day, and he liked his oatmeal and coffee hot, so I could not simply retrieve the items ahead of time. I felt like I was still babysitting.

The Epitome of Corporate America had strict rules against assistants doing personal things for their bosses. But clearly this did not stop Former Mormon or the Three-headed Dog from making demands. One day I had to babysit Former Mormon's two kids between the end of my workday and a work dinner for our department. The dinner was in TriBeCa, so I took the kids to a park there to get them out of the office and use up some energy. I constantly asked the kids if they had to go to the bathroom, and they always denied the need, but the six year old wet her pants any way. I was at a loss as to what to do. Their father lived in New Jersey, so it wasn't like we could just get a quick cab to their apartment to change.

I had no choice but to take the kids to the children's clothing boutique across from the park. I had to buy French underwear and a $60 skirt (the cheapest) for the kid. I thought for sure their dad would just pay me back. When I told him what had happened, he said that he would. The next day, I told him how much it was, and he refused. He said he was not paying $60 for the skirt, and that I had to take it back. I could not take it back because his daughter had worn the item out of the store. The owner knew what had happened and was not going to accept merchandise that had been worn. I could not believe he was trying to get me to pay for this skirt when I was not the one who had wet my pants or who had forgotten to pack extra clothes just in case. I only got paid if I was working, and this guy who had a very nice salary was refusing to reimburse me for making sure his daughter was not walking around in urine-soaked clothes all night.

As the leaves fell from the trees, my confidence fell from my body. Fall was turning into winter, and I was falling apart. My work life was miserable. The bitch was constantly on the warpath and had taken all of my extra responsibilities away. I was left with nothing but taking care of her and Former Mormon. The final leaf that was holding on for dear life fell from the tree outside the one corner of window I could see from the office in front of my cubical. That's when Three-headed Dog yelled at me for the last time. I don't even remember what she was so angry about, but it was the most absurd thing, and everyone in the office agreed with me. If I hadn't been leaving early that day to go out of town, I would have walked out the door that second never to return.

I was still shaking with anger as I called my mom on the way to the airport to tell her about Three-headed Dog's latest freak out. Three-headed Dog had no right to jeopardize my career. She had no right to treat me like a child. During my trip, I had a lot of time to think. I decided life was too short to get bitched at on an hourly basis—especially without any benefits. I had plenty of free time at work, since my responsibilities had been swept away like decaying leaves in the wind.

I vowed to be in a new job within a month and began my search for job postings. I contacted recruiters and emailed friends for leads. I decided I would not take a position if it did not offer healthcare. I carefully scheduled interviews around my time at work. Three weeks later, I had two job offers. The job I wanted most needed me to start the next day. This time I was the one who called a meeting with Three-headed Dog and Former Mormon. I told them I had received two job offers and that I'd accepted a full-time position in PR that offered benefits. "By the way, I start tomorrow," I said. They could not believe that I was in demand. I was so happy to be getting out of hell guarded by the Three-headed Dog.

I really can't remember all the ways Three-headed Dog was terrible to me. I don't think the specifics really matter. One thing that sticks in my mind is a time she was yelling at someone on the phone. She had her door open as usual. Through my unavoidable eavesdropping, I realized that the person on the other end of the line was not a naughty reporter but someone with the Disney Cruise Line. I could not tell what she was so upset about at first. Then I realized that she was yelling at this poor phone operator because the cruise line did not have a babysitter for her infant so that she could go to dinner every night with her family. She had plenty of money to afford to bring her nanny, but she was too cheap for that. She instead yelled at someone who was only doing his or her job and was only giving her information. She yelled and yelled, trying to get that person to change the situation. When she realized she wasn't going to get her way, she slammed the phone down. The entire office had heard her yelling. Several people had come out of their own offices to see what the commotion was about, and they had even asked me if I would shut her door. I knew her yelling on the phone was once again her way of asserting herself over the rest of the office and trying to show us how rich she was. There was no way I was going to shut her door only to get yelled at later. If she had wanted her door shut, she could have shut it herself. It was not worth risking my life over.

I don't think the specifics of her hatred toward me are things I would want to remember. There are holes in my memory due to illness, so I can't anyway. My body is also protecting itself from those memories I have blocked out. I used to take one step out the door of the building at the end of the day and pick up my phone to call my mom and immediately burst into tears. When it happened every day for a month, I knew I had to get out. It was not going to get any better.

Some days I did not have time to leave the office building for lunch. I would cower in my cubicle, thankful that I was short enough to dodge her verbal blows. If I chose to peek my head out, I could see my smiling co-worker in his office across from me, or catch a glimpse of the outside world through the corner of window or on his little TV usually tuned to CNBC.

On the days Three-headed Dog was in the office, I could tell she was coming the second I heard her security card beep. The opening of the door to our floor brought an even bigger sucking sound of air as the secure door opened and banged shut. It sucked a little bit of the life out of me each day she walked in. My cube faced away from the door, and I could feel her evil stare burning into my back.

Her flip-flops smacked into her feet as she shuffled behind and then past me. "Good morning," she would say flatly.

"Morning," I would reply. She did not deserve the word "good" spoken to her, and I wondered if when it crossed her lips it stung her mouth.

There were days when I prayed for an errand or a photo shoot to get me out and away from her. Many times when I had no break and I was about to break her or myself, I leapt out of my cube and declared I was going for coffee. I practically ran down the street to the safety of Starbucks two blocks away. I needed the bitter sweetness of an iced soy latte in my mouth to balance out. At times I was so mad the heat of my hand caused the cup to sweat immediately. The fresh air and exercise usually helped me get through those last few hours of the workday.

I was given a project that she had shirked in the past—like so many other assignments. I was very successful with it, and I loved working with reporters beyond taking messages. I was working with my smiling co-worker in the office in front of my cube. Suddenly, my smiling co-worker began adding more work to my plate. Three-headed Dog got so angry one day because I was on the phone supervising an interview with the *New York Times* and could not pick up her phone line when her father called. Neither of the other two useless assistants would answer. We could never let a call go to voicemail, and I had been given strict instructions that I had to answer when her father called because she would never ever speak to him on the phone. My work on that project was the first to go because her jealously of my success and her inability to deal with her personal problems took priority over team business.

After I had been gone a year from the Epitome of Corporate America, I saw Three-headed Dog and her family at the airport. I was having a hellish twenty-four hours trying to get home for Christmas. She was the last thing I needed to see. I knew I would probably strangle her if she got in my way while I was stuck for another two hours. But fate was kind and only put her there as a brief reminder of how far I had come.

It was not a moment too soon that I had two new job offers. I took the combo office manager/executive assistant job at a PR firm in midtown. I was told I could move up within a year or two. It was a young company, so it was pretty much a guarantee. Under the umbrella of the combo job, I had many other titles that had not been discussed. I ended up doing everything from breaking down boxes to organizing special events at The Four Seasons. At first, I liked the job and my co-workers. I had a lot more freedom, and the lack of micromanagement was nice. That didn't last long.

Having to prepare trip itineraries was the first step paving the long road to office hell. I don't know if my co-workers were poking at me with a stick to see if I would flinch, but I was not going to flinch. I had a lot more patience than they anticipated. I handled their busy work and their ridiculous requests without protest.

I wanted to move up in the company to do more of what I had done before, so I decided to stick it out. Maybe it was better on the other side. How wrong I was. They had originally said I could be promoted to a junior executive in the first year or two. I was the only assistant, and they promised to hire an assistant to relieve some of my workload once the company grew. Instead they hired more employees above me and piled on the responsibilities. When I started at the company, there were six employees including myself. The boss said I was to assist him and the office manager first and that the other employees would have to do some things for themselves. The employees refused to help out as needed. Instead, they acted like babies when I tried to explain that I couldn't do everything for everyone at once. Clearly, I was hiding all those extra hands in my blazer. I was not an office manager or an assistant. I was running an adult day care center. I was setting up their play dates and arranging babysitters to drive them from one play date to the next. I was even making sure they had lunches to eat. If I had been asked to change their diapers and feed them, I would not have been surprised.

Since I was the only one who would answer the phone, I had to ask to use the restroom or leave the office to run errands or to take my lunch break. I had to make sure the phones were covered. This made me feel like a prisoner rather than an employee. I tried to find a way around it, but nothing worked. I always answered on the first ring, so I figured an easy plan B would be to let the junior executives know that if the phone rang three times that meant I had likely run to the bathroom and someone should try to pick up the phone. They refused. Instead, I didn't eat lunch until three or sometimes four. For months, I didn't leave the office at all during the day. I would spend twelve hours at my desk. My creativity went out the window along with my personal freedom. I didn't have time to think outside of the prison of the office. If I had a creative thought, I didn't have time to explore it—let alone execute it. I lost my sense of self. I became a vessel for the company's requests. They expected me to be their office robot.

I was also dealing with my illness and trying to figure out what was wrong with me. Stress was only making me feel worse. Every time I made plans after work or to have lunch with friends, I had to cancel because of a last-minute project. I thought for sure Friday nights would be safe, but even then I had to work late. I finally had a chance to hang out with a friend one Friday but had to work until almost nine. I called her on my way to the subway and sobbed while I apologized for cancelling. She told me I could not let them treat me that way, but I saw no way out. After that night, I stopped making plans with my friends altogether. I worked all week and slept all weekend, trying to recover from the long hours and the stress.

I kept telling myself that it would be worth all the shit I took and the death of my personal life if I finally got promoted to do some of the things I loved at my previous job. After a year and a half of working my ass off, I realized that they didn't care how hard I worked. Nothing was good enough for them. They were challenging me just to see how long I would last. The people who had the positions I wanted worked all the time, too, even on vacation. That was not the life I wanted. I didn't want to be a slave to my job. I didn't want to spend my hard-earned money on a beach vacation just to work from a hotel room. I did not know what the answer was, but I knew there had to be a better way.

I grew tired of my life. All I did was go to work, which made me miserable. I finally recognized the pattern and decided I needed a change before I was burnt out for good. I needed a new job and a new city. I went to Los Angeles to see if I liked it there and surprisingly, I loved it. I was making plans to move when I found out I had Lyme Disease. It would require at least a year of expensive treatment, and I had to stay put. I couldn't change my insurance after the diagnosis. I had to stay until I got better. I was so discouraged. It would be hard to get better when I could not change my job, which did its part in making my illness so much worse. If I left my job, I could not afford Cobra to keep my insurance, and because of my preexisting condition, I could not get new insurance. My medical bills were so expensive, and insurance didn't cover a lot of the treatment anyway. I was not sure how I was going to pay for everything with the paycheck I was getting. There was no way I could live on anything less. I was trapped.

I let my boss know that I was sick and that it would really help if we could hire a part-time assistant or an intern for our growing office. He refused and gave me new responsibilities instead that led to even more time at the office. It was a very difficult year. My hormones were so out of whack, and I was having trouble getting up in the morning. I spiraled even more into myself.

I needed time to rest and relax. My doctor said I had to go to bed by ten at the latest every night. I needed time to prepare all my medications and make sure I took them on time. That was hard to do when I was living life as the office slave. The more people we had at the office, the more hours I had to be there. Deep down I knew I was not going to get better unless I started taking care of myself.

One day I realized that two or three years of working as an assistant had turned into four. I did not want to be an assistant for the rest of my life. I had not even had time to be creative on the side like I had originally planned. I wanted to write. I had a few book ideas that had been brewing for a while, but I never had enough time to get started. I wanted to explore photography and video arts. I had always been creative. Somehow, my whole life, I had found a way to fit in little pockets of creativity. I didn't even have a life. I had been working my butt off to make enough money to pay for my treatments and keep my insurance for a year after my diagnosis. Since Corporate America had taken over my life, I'd lost those moments. I needed to express myself creatively or I was going to explode. I knew this lifestyle was holding me back from complete recovery. I was doing a lot better and was off my medications, but there was a lot of room for improvement. My doctor told me I had to change my lifestyle if I was going to continue on the path towards better health. I realized I was never going to be promoted from my office manager/assistant position, and I didn't want to be. There was no reason to live in New York if I didn't have the energy to enjoy it. I would have to give up my insurance, and I knew chances were great I would not be able to get insurance again since I had a preexisting condition. I did not know what I would do, but I knew that continuing to live that life would only make me sick again. So I gave my notice and moved home to Nashville.

I looked out the window from the plane at the little city that was my hometown. Nashville had always seemed so big to me while growing up. Ever since the first trip back home after moving to New York, it had begun to look smaller and smaller. I wondered what my life would be like back home in Nashville after spending more than a decade in New York City. There was a blank slate in front of me. I had some ideas, but for the first time in my life I was happy about the possibility of the unknown.

It was a scary thing to leave New York after eleven years of living there, but I was ready for a fresh start. The plane landed in Nashville, and I was almost knocked over by the August humidity when I walked up the jet way. I slid back into my slight Southern accent. Three different sets of live music greeted me on the way to the baggage claim. The banjos and acoustic guitars were welcoming me back. I could not wait to see what happened next. It was scary, but it was the right choice. There are so many things I love to do, and I realized life is too short to spend it doing something you hate. I was ready to get back to my roots and find a career I loved.

## MISSING MY MATE
### *Winter 2002*

I have always been fascinated by how little things in our lives make such big waves. I remember when the first moment washed over me, changing my life forever. Wearing no makeup and holding a handful of garlic cloves, I looked across the room and saw Bruce in January of 2002. We stared at each other, and in that instant I fell in love. I had initially met Bruce at my first New York apartment. He was helping my roommate Ben move in, and I thought he was cute. We all went to see a midnight movie after unloading the van Ben had rented from U-Haul. Bruce and I could not stop talking as we bounced around in the dark in the back of the empty van on the way to the movies. I saw him a few weeks later when I was making dinner at a friend's apartment. She had invited Bruce over. I had hit my head pretty hard that day and maybe lost some sense in the process. When Bruce walked in the door, my heart fell hard.

Our similar senses of humor made us fast friends. We loved British comedies, memoirs, and Alfred Hitchcock. We were obsessed with good storytelling no matter the form. I loved to tell him stories, and he was one of the few people in my fast-paced, New York life that listened with intensity and remembered what I had to say. He would ask questions and laugh at my wit. We discussed movie ideas and obsessed over plot twists, cinematography, and editing. We flirted constantly, but it was a big joke. I acted like I was making a joke with my flirtation because I was so worried about rejection. I was not sure I could handle him not liking me back. I did not want to ruin our friendship. I thought there was no way he could be interested in me romantically. The more I knew about him the more I loved him. Secretly, I wanted him to love me back, but I settled for friendship at first.

I asked our good friend Ben if Bruce thought I was cute. "Bruce doesn't like girls. He's asexual," he said. I was confused. Bruce had been engaged before, but his fiancée had broken his heart, and he had not dated since. Still I didn't believe that he was asexual. I expected Ben to say that Bruce couldn't resist me and was going to ask me out soon. I thought I was getting signals from him. Ben's words about Bruce being asexual did not feel right, but I didn't think Ben would lie.

I grew closer to Bruce. He made me laugh like no one else. I can't remember what he said that would make me laugh, but I remember how I felt different with him. I remember the way his face stayed expressionless when he told me jokes. His deadpan delivery and quick wit made me fall even further. He rarely became animated, but when he was telling a funny story, his face would come alive as he imitated the people he was talking about. If he did not like someone, I could tell by the way he screwed his face up and talked in a whiney voice. All I wanted was to be near him.

Our friendship grew like no other I'd had with a guy before. I could tell him anything, and he accepted me just as I was. He loved my sassy side. It often pushed others away, but it only brought him closer. I loved how quiet he was, how he listened and remembered. He was always happy to see me. I hoped he would see how I felt about him, but despite our constant flirting and innuendo, I sensed that the chemistry was still a just a joke to him. He never seemed serious about what he was saying. He would always laugh nervously or say that he was just kidding.

We had been friends for a while, and then out of nowhere, he had a girlfriend. I knew he had been hanging out with this girl because they had worked together. I did not know they had fallen for each other. My apartment with Ben served as the party house and the meeting place. I was excited that Bruce was coming over since I had not seen him much. When he arrived, Ben started teasing him right away about how he was dating Mary. I did not believe it at first. Then, hoping it was just another joke, I asked Bruce if he really was dating Mary. He very quietly admitted it was true. I didn't know who to be angrier at when I heard the news: Ben for lying about Bruce being asexual, this girl for getting in my way, or Bruce for not noticing what was right in front of him. I prayed I could make it through the night. I had to hang out with them without tears or telling off one of the three. I smiled and said they were a cute couple. I'd missed my chance, but it was my own fault. My mind was constantly spinning on the merry-go-round of opportunities I'd had in the past to tell him how I felt about him. But I was too scared to share my real feelings for him. If I could barely handle loving him in secret, I had no idea how I could keep my heart from bursting open if the love was returned. I could not imagine a world without him. What if I had come clean about my feelings and he had rejected me? I could not help but wonder what else Ben had told me about Bruce was untrue. I felt like *Alice in Wonderland*—no longer knowing which way was up.

I hated myself for being too scared to tell Bruce how I felt. I wanted to hate him, but I loved him too much. Instead, I hated his girlfriend for taking him from me. She could never love him as much as I did. I was lucky that I did not have to see them together much. Ben, however, endlessly teased Bruce about having a girlfriend, so I heard about their relationship all the time. Somehow, I knew by Bruce's reactions to the teasing that their connection was not what he had hoped it would be. I could tell something was seriously lacking, and he did not know what to do about it. She ended it a few months later. There was a strange love triangle thing going on with her ex-husband and Bruce. I did not understand it, but I was happy she was gone. Despite the new opportunity, I was still afraid to tell him how I felt. If he liked me, he would have told me by then. I couldn't help loving him, but I didn't believe he would return the love.

Right before Valentine's Day, about four years since I had first met Bruce, my therapist asked if I was secretly in love with any of my friends. She had asked me about this before, but I had denied it. No one knew how I felt about him. A huge grin spread across my face, and I blushed.

"Well, there is someone I like, but I've never told him," I confessed. I told her about Bruce and how I had been in love with him for four years but had never done anything about it besides pretend to flirt.

"I am not supposed to tell you what to do, but I really think you should tell him," she said.

"Really? You really think I should tell him?" I asked.

"Yes, I really think you should try."

I said I would think about it. Suddenly I could think of nothing else. What if he didn't feel the same way? What if I freaked him out and he didn't want to be friends anymore? I decided life couldn't wait any longer. I would have to let go of the unknown and deal with whatever I got. I invited him over the weekend before Valentine's Day.

The night came. I hadn't seen him in weeks, and I tried to hide my nervous shaking. I had no idea how to tell him how I felt. For once my words were of no help at all. We were watching TV, and I had the idea to give him Valentine's Day conversation hearts. I picked out specific phrases, but he ate them without reading. I started to read them to him. I hoped he would finally see that I was not joking. I tried to be nonchalant at first, and then I kicked the flirting into high gear. I was terrified but had to get my point across. When that didn't work, I handed him a heart that said "true love." I looked him right in the eye and made him read it out loud. He sat up a little bit, and I could see the recognition on his face.

"Wait, you're serious, aren't you?" he said.

I couldn't hide the shaking anymore. It felt as if the world had stopped spinning. I waited a second and said, "Yes."

"But you can't like me because I like you," he said.

"What? You like me?"

"I've always liked you."

He kissed me. It was like I had never been fully alive until that moment. My senses soaked up the acceptance they had longed for. He was mine. I woke up the next day with an instant smile on my face. I could not contain my excitement when he later said he'd always wanted to marry me. I was thrilled. I always knew he was the one, and I felt like the stars had finally aligned. I had waited a long time for the right person. I wanted my first time to be with the one I loved. A few weeks later, the wait was over. He was my first.

After a blissful first three months together, Bruce got sick. He had been sick before—in and out of the hospital for a time—but thought he was better. This time was worse. He was not the most social person I knew, but he became even more withdrawn, not leaving his apartment and not letting me see him. I could not help but worry about him, but I knew we could get through it together if he would just let me help him. He was in the hospital, and I tried to visit him, but he did not want me to see him in the state he was in. I felt guilty because I was secretly relieved that I could not see him. I was not sure I could handle seeing him in the hospital hooked up to machines and looking pale and thin. My heart had suffered enough just waiting for him to love me. I could not handle the pain of seeing him in pain. Not long after he left the hospital, he called. I was excited to hear from him and hoped we could make a plan to see each other soon. I could tell from his tone that was not why he was calling.

"I can't put you through this," he said.

"Put me through what?" I asked. My heart started to swell.

"I can't put you through me being sick and being in and out of the hospital. I can't be in a relationship right now."

I sat upright in my lounge chair. "But we finally got

together," I said. "We just started dating."

"I can't do it. You will hate me for it. I can't be the person I want to be for you right now."

I was stunned. This was not where I thought things were going. I thought we could work through this. I knew it would not be easy, but I had to find a way to change his mind. My mouth started moving as quickly as it could. "But you are my person. I can't let go of you. There is no one else out there for me. We waited so long and we just started. How can it be over already?"

"I can't do it."

I had no words left. He said goodbye, and I burst into tears. I did not know how I was going to go on without him. He had been by my side for so long, even though we had only been dating for a short time.

I knew that his ex-fiancée had cheated on him while he was in the hospital. I could later understand his apprehension, but I did not want to break up. I wanted to be there for him. I stared at the phone in my hand. It was like someone had turned off the light switch, and I was lost in the dark—like I was running to an open door, only to smack into glass. I had finally found my man—my other half—and now it was over. I did not know what to do without him. I did not know where to begin to pick up the pieces around me.

I was lost without him. A few days after Bruce broke up with me, my dog was attacked in the dog park and almost died. I did not know who to call or who could help comfort me while I was sitting at the veterinary hospital waiting to find out if my dog was going to be okay or not. The only person I could think of was Bruce. I called him, and he arrived within fifteen minutes. He was there for me while I cried and worried. He sat with me for hours until I was told Neville was going to be okay and they were going to keep him over night. I knew I could still at least be friends with him. If I ever needed him, he would be there. No matter what.

Bruce was very sick. He had been in the hospital again

and wouldn't let me see him. I thought he was going to die. I didn't know how I could live without him. His life started to revolve around doctors' appointments. It was hard for him to live in New York by himself, so he moved to Maine where his mother lived. I didn't hear from him for months. I was so worried that he had died and that no one had told me. Then one day in late winter, he called. He had been in and out of the hospital again. He went to the hospital one day, found out he had colon cancer, and had to have emergency surgery to remove his colon. Then he found out he had diabetes. He was in the hospital for a few months. After the surgery, he felt better than before. He was going to need some time to heal, but he thought he might be able to lead a normal life.

I held onto this hope like a pigeon holds onto a scrap of bagel when a sparrow starts creeping in. We talked on the phone more often. It was so nice to hear his voice after silence for so long. We eased back into friendship and once again buried our love for one another in our conversations. At first we did not joke and flirt like we had before. I was hesitant to goof around after worrying about him for so long and enduring the devastating break up. But after a while, we went back to our joking and flirting. I was so nervous, putting myself out there again.

I had tried to get over him without success. I tried to date other people. He told me he did not want me missing out on life just because he had to. I had a few notable relationships over the years and even more notable terrible dates. I met a few guys, who I thought might make good relationship material, but they ended up being jerks. For the most part, I was just alone. I lived my life to the fullest on my own. It was like I was in a relationship incubator waiting for either my heart to be healed so I could love again or for Bruce to get well so we could be together.

When Bruce and I talked on the phone, I wanted so badly to tell him that I still loved him. I tried to get him to let me move to Maine to be with him, but he wouldn't let me. He didn't want me to throw away my life for him. He didn't want me to see him going through his recovery. Cancer had been tearing through his family like a tidal wave, so he wouldn't even let me visit. He was trapped in his house for a long time trying to get well. He did not have much of a life and it was hard for him to talk to me sometimes because he did not have much to talk about. I could hear the melancholy in his voice. I tried to cheer him up, but there was not much I could do. He liked hearing about my adventures in New York, but I felt guilty living an exciting life while he was stuck on the couch.

After we had been talking again for about a year, I gathered up all my courage and admitted I still loved him. I was surprised when he said he felt the same way. He reminded me that he did not end our relationship because he didn't love me, but because he loved me too much to make me go on that journey through illness with him. I knew he felt robbed of his twenties. He'd spent most of that decade sick. He did not want to rob me of experiences. He wanted me to be free to live to the fullest for the both of us. We opened up to each other again and talked about how much we loved each other, how our relationship made us realize those things you read about in books—which we were always so skeptical about—can actually happen.

About a year later, his demeanor changed. His tone was lighter, and he started to have hope that he might be able to live his life again. He said that if he was able to move out of his mom's house, he would move to Los Angeles and not back to New York. He wanted to be a storyboard artist, and there was more work for him there. I told him he had to move back to New York so we could be together again, but I couldn't sway him. I had visited LA briefly, and it wasn't my kind of place. I loved New York just about as much as I loved Bruce. I could never leave. I was a lifer.

Another year went by without Bruce. He was still stuck in Maine. We still talked on the phone. I had brought up going to see him, or having him come to the city, but it never worked out. He said it would be too hard. If he came to see me, he wouldn't want to leave. I told him he didn't have to, but he said he couldn't let me take care of him. It wouldn't be fair to me.

If we couldn't be together in New York, I had to know what I thought about living in LA. It turned out my dad was going to be there for a couple weeks on a business trip. Perfect timing. I rented a convertible for a day and a half so that my dad and I could drive up the Pacific coast. We got up early Saturday morning and drove to Santa Monica. I walked out to the ocean alone to take pictures. It was quiet and unpopulated with only the sound of the ocean and the seagulls. I came over a little hill of sand and saw the ocean. A wave crashed against the sand, tears came to my eyes, and in that moment, my gut screamed that I had to move across the country, with or without Bruce. I knew not to ignore my gut. It was what got me to New York from Nashville, and it had never steered me wrong. But my head still wasn't sure. I decided if I found a shoe, I would know I had to move to LA.

One day, years ago, I'd found a lone Jimmy Choo in the snow in Brooklyn. I had my camera with me and took some pictures. A couple days later, I found another single shoe, and a few days after that, another. I took pictures of each. Ever since, I have found single shoes and other odd, lost items ranging from an embroidered vintage handkerchief on 42nd Street to a pair of $200 jeans over a parking meter on West Broadway. I often find lone shoes when I am discouraged or questioning my path. When I find them, I always take pictures and consider it a sign I am on the right track. If I hadn't been walking down that particular street, at that particular time, I wouldn't have found that shoe. I knew that if I found a shoe in LA, I would know it was where I needed to be.

My dad and I walked around Santa Monica. I could see myself living there, riding my bike to the beach every day. It was so laid-back and calm. After ten years living the fast pace of my favorite city, slowing down was a refreshing concept. I looked everywhere for a shoe but found none.

We drove up the PCH. There was not a cloud to be found, and the ocean sparkled silver in the sun. I wanted to keep going to Malibu, but we had to turn around to return the car before noon. I sat in the passenger seat of my dad's car after returning mine and looked out the window. Suddenly, I was shouting and opening the door. "There's a shoe! There's a shoe!" I jumped out before my dad could start the car. I took pictures and got back in. I couldn't believe it happened so fast. Still worried about making such a big leap, I decided I needed to find another lone shoe, just to be sure.

The next night, I convinced my dad to go to Spago with me. The food was amazing and the atmosphere was so relaxed. Not at all like the sometimes stiff, upscale restaurants in New York.

My dad went to the restroom, and when he got back, he said, "You have to go around the corner."

"Why? Is Barbra Streisand there?"

"No. I'm not going to tell you. You just have to go around the corner."

My dad was not one to keep things to himself. I knew it had to be something special. I walked around the corner and stopped dead. There were six shelves on the wall and a row on the floor of single, unpaired vintage shoes. I fished through my purse to find the camera I take everywhere. I fell more in love with LA with every step. If this wasn't enough confirmation that it was where I needed to be, I don't know what would have been. I had forty-nine reasons to move to LA right in front of me.

I returned to New York, and it wasn't the same. For the first time, I was not happy to be home. I went to my favorite places, but the excitement was gone. All I could think about was what my life in LA would be like and when I could go back.

I called Bruce. I was so excited to tell him about my plans to move. I wanted to be there first so I could establish myself and be ready for when he was finally able to join me in LA.

"I went to LA over the weekend," I told him. "I did not think I would like it, but I absolutely love it. I am looking for a job there because I want to move there as soon as possible. LA feels like the place where I am meant to live." I expected him to be excited after me begging him to move back to New York for so long. Instead, he was silent. I continued, "I want to make sure you know I am doing this for myself. I am moving there with or without you."

His sober tone killed my enthusiasm. He said, "I understand. I would love to move out there, but now I am having very expensive dental problems. I don't think I will ever be able to move out of my mom's house—let alone move to LA."

"But I thought maybe we could finally be together. I thought I could move out there first and get established, and then you could meet me there. I thought this was the answer." I had no more words to help state my case.

"I do not see it happening."

"Okay. Goodbye."

I had been walking in my neighborhood while we were talking, but after our conversation, I came to a halt between two large buildings that blocked out all the light on the sunny day. I was in the dark. I did not know what to do. I did not know where to go. I just stood still with all the hope knocked out of my heart.

It was over. I had finally found a way we could be together, but just like the waves roll in, they roll back out. I had become one of my beloved shoes. Lost and missing my mate. Bruce had been swept away, and now the waves of LA were crashing over my love affair with New York.

The hope for LA did not last long either. Three days later, I had my diagnosis of Lyme Disease, and I was stuck in New York until I got better. I had to deal with my own serious health issues over the next year. I was incredibly distracted by my sickness, but I was still unsuccessful in pushing Bruce completely from my mind. I had a new understanding of his life and struggles with illness. I did call him once, and he actually picked up the phone. It made me feel like Barbra Streisand in *The Way We Were*. She calls Robert Redford after he breaks up with her because she is so distraught after realizing he is her only friend and the only one to understand how she feels. For days afterward, I missed him so much I just wanted to die. I decided it was too painful to talk to him. I could not call him again. We were never going to be together anyway, and I did not see the point in torturing myself.

Suffering and sadness became my new normal that year. I dreamt of living in LA while I was miserable and sick in New York. On Easter weekend I had to stay in the city and could not go home to visit my family; I could not afford plane tickets because of medical expenses. I was homesick, heartbroken, and inconsolable. I wanted to call Bruce so much my heart hurt, but I knew I could not handle the letdown if he did not answer or if he got off the phone too quickly. I locked myself up in my apartment and ignored the sunshine that was finally making an appearance after a long, cold winter. I instead listened to a folk music station on Pandora while crying to the songs that reminded me of home. Every time a song mentioned Nashville, which many did, I cried, and the slumping got worse until I was lying on my side wondering why I had to have such bad luck in life.

When Emmylou Harris's "You've Been on My Mind" played, I lifted out of my slump. She sang the exact words I wanted to say to Bruce. I did not have to talk to him. I could let her speak for me. I decided to email him a YouTube video of her singing. I knew he would understand every word of her song, but I didn't know if he would respond.

A few days later, I had a bad fall and almost broke my back. I was rushing to get to work, walking on the uneven cobblestone around my building. My ankle gave out, and I fell off the curb in front of a cab. I landed on my knees. Then my heavy backpack slid forward toward my head and smashed my face into the sidewalk. The momentum that threw my head forward to the pavement sent my feet flying off the curb. My feet landed on the ground in front of my head. I felt the vertebra in my lower back rubbing together and almost snap as my body "scorpioned" forward, but my feet went back the other way, saving my spine. Thankfully I did not get run over by the cab. A neighbor, along with the people on the full M80 bus, saw me fall. My neighbor helped me up and pulled me out of the way. She put an ice pack to my swollen nose and sent me to the emergency room.

The impact had cracked my nose and broken my fragile spirit. The panic from the fall had loosened up my stuffed emotions. The doctor sent me home with instructions to rest. I spent the day in bed trying to do as much work as I could between crying fits.

My spirits instantly lifted after I saw Bruce's name in my inbox. I would have jumped up and down if I could have stood up on my injured leg long enough. Instead, I exclaimed to my dog that Bruce had emailed me. I was nervous to see what his response would be. I hoped for the best and began to read.

Bruce had written that he'd been thinking of me when I'd sent him the email. He didn't want to be a voice from the past if I did not want to hear one. He said it was spooky we had been thinking about each other at the same time, and it made him wonder how many times that had happened before without us realizing it. His health was finally cooperating with him, and he was working on his storyboard portfolio with the goal of moving to LA in the fall.

His email seemed different than the ones he'd sent in the past. He seemed very chatty. I was surprised he offered so much conversation without prompting. Maybe he had been waiting for me to reach out to him. I read the email over and over, not believing it was real.

I responded and told him I was finally looking for jobs in LA—with the goal of getting my ass out there as soon as possible. Maybe we were not doomed to spend our lives apart. My own health was slowly improving, and I was looking forward to a new life, which hopefully included Bruce.

After a few months of renewed contact with Bruce, I went to LA to interview for a job I could not believe was almost mine. As I looked for apartments, I thought about the life I could start there. The promise of sunshine almost every day and the possibility of Bruce had me floating from place to place. When I did not get the position, I was devastated—not only because of the loss of a possible dream job but also because it meant I couldn't start that next step with Bruce. Over the next few weeks I fell apart. Nothing was working, and all the hope had dissipated. I was so over New York, my job, and everything. There was a memory on every street corner of the city, but they'd all turned sour and bitter. I moved home to Nashville for a fresh start.

Bruce and I became close again as I thawed out from the last few terrible months in New York. I decided to train to be a Pilates Instructor. The plan was to get my certification, make some money, and get out to LA as soon as possible. I figured it would take about two years, one to train and one to make money. I got started right away, working through my mat certifications and teaching as much as possible. Then I experienced a delay in my comprehensive training schedule. I wouldn't be able to teach private sessions in the studio with the equipment and start saving money right away.

Once again I was devastated because it had taken over a year for the comprehensive to even be on the calendar. I was behind schedule, and each delay pushed my patience. I just wanted to be finished and finally be with Bruce or at least be in LA. We were supposed to start the training in October, the same weekend my parents were going to Vermont and New Hampshire to visit my brother and his girlfriend and to check out the fall foliage. When they were originally planning the trip, they had invited me. I wanted to go along once I realized how close they would be to Bruce's house in Maine, but I had to start my training. The sooner it started, the sooner I could finish. I was devastated when I got the call saying the training was delayed for six weeks because of paperwork issues, on the other hand, I could visit Bruce. I got subs for all my classes and left.

I contacted Bruce to tell him I was heading up north, and he said he was moving to LA a week after we were coming. For once, I was just in time—we could actually see each other. One possible obstacle stood in our way, but I prayed that fate would not be so cruel to destroy a reunion.

The day came that I was supposed to see Bruce. My family kept delaying the trip from New Hampshire to Maine, and I was pissed. I also felt a little queasy at the idea of seeing him for the first time in six years since he'd left New York.

My father could not drive fast enough once we finally got on the road. I tried to read and distract myself from the anticipation, but the words were just a blur on the page. I also tried looking out the window to gaze at the changing leaves, but nothing could keep me from thinking about how close I was to Bruce.

I finally arrived at his house, and I could not believe it. It was actually happening. My heart was pounding out of my chest as I walked up to the door. It was decorated for Halloween. A sign above the door, featuring a witch's skirt, tights, and shoes, had the phrase, "The shoes are the thing." *They most certainly are,* I thought. My shaky finger rang the bell.

An eternity went by before Bruce came to the door. We immediately embraced. I could feel his heart beating just as hard as mine. We stayed there for a minute, fearing that if we let go, the other would disappear. I felt so safe in his arms. It could not be real, but the beat of his heart was my constant reminder this was not a dream. I was finally here, he was here, and we were together. He invited me in. He showed me the storyboard portfolio he had been putting together, and we reminisced about the movies he had worked on in New York. It still felt like a dream. We talked for a little while, and then he suggested some restaurants for lunch. He lived in a cute little town that reminded me of Stars Hollow on *Gilmore Girls.* As we walked to the restaurant down the street, I realized that we were on our first date. We had only dated for three months in the same city, but we had always just hung out at my house. Somehow we'd never gone out on an actual date. He even paid for my lunch. I knew he was saving for his trip and new apartment expenses, so it meant a lot to me that he wouldn't let me pay. I was so nervous, excited, and scared that I shook. I kept blinking back tears, and it was all I could do not to bawl from happiness through the first few hours we were together. He was all I wanted in this world, and I finally had him—if only for a day.

He took me for a ride after lunch in his new car. We drove all over New Hampshire and Maine, going to see a lighthouse and to the beach. He had satellite radio and let me pick the stations. I decided on sixties music. We looked at all the vacation homes along the coast. Some of the houses had names on the front like people name their boats. I thought it was strange, but Bruce said it was very common. Then I saw it. A house was proudly named "Someday Happened." I almost yelled trying to get Bruce to see. I had always told him that someday we would be together again. He never believed me, but *someday* was happening.

We were having the best day, but as it wore on, all I wanted to feel was his hand in mine. At first, I was scared and still trying to get over the fact that he was right in front of me, but by mid-afternoon, I told him that if he didn't touch me, I was going to explode. He held my hand, and before we got out of the car to go to Barnes and Noble, like we always used to, he kissed me. I had been so scared that it would not feel the same—that time and life would have erased the passion we'd once had—but I was wrong. The sun was going down. We were running out of time together.

"Bruce, we need to go somewhere we can make out. We only have a few hours left. I want to make the most of every second."

He was not as enthusiastic as I was. "Let's wait until I get to LA, and I will fly you out to visit me."

"But I can't wait that long. I need you so badly."

Humor was his next tactic. "But if we go make out somewhere in the dark, a scary man with a hook will come and kill us like in those terrible fifties horror films."

"That is not going to happen. But I might die if you don't kiss me again. I am willing to risk the hook man."

I finally won. We found a somewhat secluded parking lot where we could be alone in the dark before he had to take me back at the hotel where my parents were staying. I had changed the radio station to the fifties channel. As we pulled into the parking spot, the most clichéd, boy-meets-girl, cheesy make-out song came on. I am absolutely sure it was used in dating service commercials when I was younger. We looked at each other in disbelief. It felt like we were in a movie. We are pre-nostalgic people and were transported back in time to become 1950s teens. We laughed and asked each other if it was really happening. We decided we had to turn off the radio for fear someone would drive by and see us in the blue glow. We made out like teenagers until it was time for me to go.

I didn't have a key card to get into the lobby after hours. Bruce would not let me wait outside by myself for my dad to come let me in. I did not want him to meet my dad. My parents did not know that Bruce and I were in love, and I wanted to keep it that way. They would know when there was a reason to. My father finally came downstairs, and they shook hands. It was the first time my father had met one of my boyfriends, but he had no idea. I hugged Bruce goodbye one last time, and he left. I reveled in the glow of love for the rest of the evening. I could barely sleep, but it didn't matter because I had to get up early for my flight back to Nashville the next day.

While I was waiting at the airport, I looked online to find the song we'd heard in the car. I discovered it was "Sleepwalk" by Santo and Johnny. I downloaded it and listened to it with a smile on my face.

I arrived home and excitedly shared the story with some of my closest friends. They could not believe how romantic it was and said it sounded like a movie.

Six weeks later, at the end of December, I started my training program for Pilates, and Bruce was settling in at a friend's apartment in LA. We were both on our way to living our new lives. I decided to approach my training with all my focus. Bruce and I communicated with new enthusiasm. I did not go anywhere once my training started. The sooner I finished, the sooner I could make more money, and the sooner I could move to LA to be with Bruce. It was like a marathon to me. I wanted to do everything right, but I also just wanted to be done.

Toward the end of my training, I started to peek out of my Pilates cocoon and think about the future—about what my life might be like. I started to worry about Bruce—about how a million beautiful, seemingly perfect girls in LA were probably throwing themselves at him. There was no way I could compete with that. He started to drift away soon after. My phone calls and texts went unanswered. I did get him on the phone finally only to hear, "I'll call you back." He never did. That night, the night before my advanced test, I had a dream. I was in a helicopter looking down at a long rocky precipice by the sea. Bruce was there on the cliff. He was wearing a tuxedo, and the precipice was decorated for a wedding ceremony. I saw him standing in the receiving line next to a woman in a powder blue dress. I just knew that it was his wedding and that the woman was his wife. The helicopter slowly ascended higher into the sky as my hopes fell into the ocean. In the next part of the dream, I was with my friend Morgan. It was the middle of the night, and we were in a beach house—probably in the Hamptons. A bunch of ridiculous surfer-type dudes that were hanging around kept hitting on me, but it was kind of a joke. I looked at Morgan after the last one had taken his half-assed shot at me and said, "Is this all that's left? Is this what I have to deal with if I can't have Bruce?" She just looked at me and sighed.

I did not hear from Bruce, and a month later I called him and left a message. He didn't call me back, but I had another dream. This time I was in an office, and it seemed like I owned it. Bruce came to visit, and he had not only his wife with him but also his two kids. I was devastated as they rounded the corner and I saw the children. It was incredibly awkward as I showed him around. But I was proud of what I had to show him and that he'd cared enough to show up.

I finally finished my training in September and passed my final test with flying colors. My original plan was to go to LA and visit Bruce as soon as I was done with the training, but there was too much going on. He had promised me in Maine that he would fly me out to see him. In November, I sent him a text to see if I could come visit him in December. I needed to see what LA felt like after a few years in Nashville, which had turned out to be much better than I'd anticipated. I needed to see what it felt like to be with Bruce again. I needed to know if I should work toward moving or stay in Nashville—at least for a few more years. He was not going to be in LA when I wanted to go. I was lying in bed on a break from teaching for the afternoon. His responses were not what I expected.

I got a wild hair in me, and the safety of my bed gave me the courage to ask him the most important question. I decided to text him.

"Do you still love me?"

"What?"

I almost threw my phone across the room in my rage at his words. How could he respond with that? Instead of giving it to him, I waited an hour. I gave myself time to cool off and come up with a clear-headed answer.

I responded, "Very helpful answer thanks."

I had my answer. I knew the score.

He wrote back something about how I had a lot going for me and I should focus on that. He was at work and couldn't talk. I wanted to say that all I wanted to add to my life was him, but instead I stayed silent. I felt like the wind had been knocked out of me. I knew it was over for good. The salt water of my tears would have to serve as my ocean now.

I will never know what was happening with Bruce in LA, but I had a feeling that he was slowly losing interest in me. I was too busy getting my Pilates certification to notice. He never gave me a reason for his abrupt end to things. I never asked for one either. I finally saw that if it had not happened in eleven years, it was never going to happen. I have not spoken to him since.

## STUCK IN THE MUD
*Summer 2002*

I had my first date with JP. I was so excited!

I had met him at a party in Nashville that my friend Lucy had invited me to. I was home for about a month in the summer and was trying to see as many friends as possible. I had been to a concert earlier that evening, so I was dressed up. I was wearing my black satin corset and my black-and-white striped star skirt. I looked cute. I had been outside talking to all the guys, and then Lucy and I went inside to get a drink. We sat down at the kitchen table, and she said, "Okay, you need to tell me which guy you want to give your number to because they are all fighting over you."

I was a little surprised. "Really? Which guys?" Guys didn't really ask me out, and they definitely did not fight over me. I knew my corset had special powers, but I wasn't aware of this one.

She described them in order of tallest to shortest. I was terrible at remembering names, but I never forgot a face.

"Colin, the tall, skinny bleach blond with glasses, is creative and likes video editing just like you," she said.

"I liked talking to him, but I don't think I am attracted to him."

"Next is JP," she said. "He is Colin's best friend. He was the cute blond you were talking to in the kitchen."

"Yeah, I remember him," I said, raising my eyebrows. "I will probably let him have my number, but continue with the list."

She listed the guys who were stoners and then the slackers, but I wasn't really paying attention. I was thinking about JP and how much I wanted to go out on a date with him.

Once she made it to the end of the list, I laughed and said, "Well, they can all ask for my number. It doesn't mean they will actually get it."

I picked JP. I already thought he was cute. We'd had a conversation at his kitchen table for about an hour after hanging out with all the guys outside.

Somehow we got on the topic of sounds in the night.

JP said, "I almost called the police in the middle of the night a few months ago because I thought there was someone in the house. It turned out that my parents got an icemaker and forgot to tell me."

I was thinking to myself about how sensitive I was to sounds in the night. I wanted to echo his thoughts, but I didn't want him to think I was crazy. I remained cool but surprised and said, "Oh really?"

He instead echoed my thoughts and said, "I am really a sensitive person, especially to sounds in the night. The littlest thing can make me scared. I still don't understand why my parents got an ice machine and did not tell me about it."

I decided it was safe to open up about my own feelings on this subject. "I know how you feel. Sometimes I have trouble sleeping, and the littlest sound can be terrifying. It's funny that you mention the icemaker. I don't have an icemaker in my apartment in New York, but my parents do here. It scared the crap out of me the other night when the machine was shifting the ice around. It's funny how something so small as a cube or two of ice can sound as loud and scary as an intruder in the middle of the night."

He laughed. "It's funny how we both feel the same way about something like this."

"I have never talked about how scared I get at night sometimes from the littlest sounds," I said.

"Me either."

I did not have a lot of experience with guys, but this was the first time that I felt comfortable with a guy who I thought was cute. I felt like I could be myself. I knew we were connecting on some other level. I was very excited that he thought so, too.

Before I left, JP asked for my number. I gave it to him, and he said we should go out sometime. I agreed. I was ecstatic as I left the party. I did not have many guys asking for my number or asking me out on dates in New York. I decided I should get dressed up more often.

About a week later, JP asked me out. I didn't want him to drive all the way out to my neighborhood, so I told him to pick me up from my friend Lana's house. She helped me get ready for my date. Plucking eyebrows is her secret talent, and she also helped me with my make-up.

We went to dinner at Carraba's. I had not been on many dates before, so I was nervous but not for long. It was easy to talk to him. I told him about how my friends and I had almost been arrested for playing on a playground the week before. He thought it was hilarious that someone as sweet and innocent-looking as myself could almost be arrested—especially for playing on a playground. After dinner he said he was taking me to a playground where we wouldn't get arrested.

The rain had pummeled Nashville all week but had finally stopped the day before. JP helped me out of the car and into the darkness. I looked cute in my little black flowered dress with my super adorable pink slip-on sandals from Pearl River Mart. We started to walk to the swings. I noticed the grass was a little marshy from the rain. I was worried about the mud. "I'm a New Yorker," I said. "I don't like nature." I was trying not to complain, but I knew my shoes weren't up for the muddy wet grass. He said he would go ahead of me and make sure it wasn't too muddy. He made it to the swings and encouraged me to keep going.

I took tentative steps, knowing it wasn't a good idea. I took a few more steps, and then my right foot fell in a hole—

a seriously muddy hole. "Oh no! My shoe, my shoe! I'm stuck, I'm stuck."

JP came running to my side and helped me get my foot out of the hole. It was covered in mud.

"Oh no! What am I going to do? What about my shoe?"

He carried me to his car. "I'll go get your shoe," he said. So he put me in the seat and went off to dig.

He returned with my muddy slip-on. I sighed, thinking it was ruined. He gave me a bunch of tissues to clean my foot and leg off, and he started to clean my shoe. The mud was not coming off easily, so he took me back to his house and got Q-tips. He rinsed my shoe off with the hose and then came back to the car to clean it out with the Q-tips. I couldn't believe it. He felt so bad about getting me stuck in the mud, but we laughed at how ridiculous it was. He said we'd go somewhere that didn't involve nature, and headed to Café Coco.

JP and I had a good time together. We went out on a few more dates and had a lot of fun. One particular date stands out. We went to play mini golf one summer afternoon. It was a beautiful day. The place also had go-carts and an arcade. I guess we were nervous, but we played our round quickly. Then we went to the arcade. It was deserted, so we had our pick of games. They had Skee-Ball, and I have always considered myself pretty good at that game. We got a ton of quarters and played side-by-side, competing with each other. I beat his score most of the time. We were racking up tickets, and then I did so well with one game that I broke the machine. I had to move over to the other side of JP.

We were laughing and comparing our techniques, and then we ran out of quarters. I was going on about something nervously when he turned around and started walking toward me. I wasn't sure what to do, so I walked backward away from him. I did not realize there was a pool table behind me. Even with my slow steps backward and his slow steps forward, it did not take long for me to bump into the table. He continued to get closer, and I continued to talk nervously.

He leaned in toward my face and stopped me midsentence with my first real kiss.

I was stunned. I felt a flutter in my heart and my stomach like I never had before. He continued to kiss me, and I became limp in his arms. He stopped, and I opened my eyes wide, still surprised at what had happened. It took me a minute to regain my senses. "Wow. I guess that's one way to get me to stop talking," I said.

"I've been waiting to do that."

"You did well," I said, still stunned.

It felt like I was floating on air for a few days afterward. Every time I saw a kiss on television I thought back to that moment. I felt the flutter. I couldn't wait to do it again.

I called my friend Lucy, the one who had set us up, to tell her the news.

"I know. JP told me," she said.

I talked to her about how I felt about him, how much I liked him, how I was excited to see where things went.

"He has some weird thing with his ear and he can't ever get his ear wet," Lucy said.

"That means he can't go swimming and has to be very careful about showers and stuff."

She knew how much I loved to swim and go to the beach. I wondered why she was trying to deter me.

"It's going to be really painful when you go back to New York and can't see him," she continued.

They were very good friends. I knew this already. She did have a point, but I still really liked him a lot. I wanted to make the most out of the next few weeks I had to spend with him. I had a feeling that something else was going on. I suspected that Lucy had begun to realize that she had feelings for JP, too.

I hung out with JP some more until I went back to New York. We had a good time, and I was sad to leave him, but it was for the best. Lucy confessed to me later that she did have feelings for JP. I guess it took me being in her way for her to finally realize it and do something about it.

## ALMOST ARRESTED
*Summer 2002*

I have always wanted to be seen as a good girl. I needed people to have that image of me. I was raised to follow the rules. I have a lot of respect of for some rules—the ones I feel keep me safe. Then there are the rules I think are stupid and just asking to be broken. I also have a talent for getting into trouble for following the rules. The more closely and to a T I follow the rules, the more I get into trouble. And if Zoe is with me, the consequences are usually worse.

As a teen, I was ambitious and already had an entertainment career. When I had free time to hang out with my friends, we did not have time for rule breaking. We really just wanted to release stress. I didn't have a curfew because my parents trusted me. I had a career and had to be responsible. If I felt like I was out too late, I would call my parents and let them know I was spending the night. These sleepovers were completely innocent, except for maybe the gossip sessions. We spent our evenings playing board games like Disney Trivia or The Barbie Game or listening to music and bitching about ballet.

We weren't tempted to drink because we had to get up early the next day and dance either in class or at the Tennessee Performing Arts Center. Some of the other girls in our classes were grumpy on Saturday mornings because they were hungover. The vices among my friends and I, however, were cookies or chips and salsa. I did not even drink until I was in college and was eighteen years old. I was a bartender at

*The Lion King* on Broadway and had no interest in the liquor I had full access to. The first drink I ever had was an accident. I had attended the premiere of the made-for-TV movie version of *Annie*. There was a party afterward. When we arrived, they offered us eggnog or wine. I said no at first but when approached again I didn't want to seem rude. I took eggnog not realizing it had rum in it. I took one sip and exclaimed to my friend, "That's terrible! What's in that?"

"There's probably rum in it." She said nonchalantly.

"Oh no! I drank alcohol!" I was appalled and discarded the awful drink. I had conflicting feelings swimming around in my head. I wondered if the servers would actually give me a glass of wine if I wanted one. I doubted I looked twenty-one. I wondered what wine tasted like. The good girl on my shoulder told me to let it go and move on. The daredevil on the other shoulder kept nagging me to try it. I decided to try a sip of my friend's wine. I didn't really like it. I was so tipsy from those two sips it was all I could do not to go ask Uncle Jessie, John Stamos, to dance with me and to keep from telling thirteen-year-old Lindsay Lohan how much I loved her in *The Parent Trap*.

I did not care for the drinks, and when I told my roommates what had happened, they decided I was going to drink with them at our friend's Christmas party in a few months. I told them no but eventually succumbed to the peer pressure and had a White Russian that I nursed all evening.

Later in college, I realized that when I played by the rules, I got into trouble, so I might as well have a good time. If that good time involved breaking some rules, it wasn't the end of the world. When I broke the rules, no one bothered me. I used to think that I had to behave, but that usually did not work out. So now I am a little more lenient with myself. I enjoy life, and if I follow the rules and get into trouble, I at least have a good story to tell.

One summer after I had turned twenty-one, I went home from New York to Nashville for a month.

My friends in Nashville were mostly younger than me.

We had to get creative with our time out of the house since none of them were old enough to go to late-night establishments for music, dancing, or whatever. Zoe and I had a serious coffee addiction; we spent much of our time in coffee shops throughout the city. We liked to visit them all.

They all have their different perks. Café Coco has a great back porch. It is a bitch to find parking—especially for someone who is parallel parking challenged, such as myself— but we really like it there. They have good options for drinks that don't involve caffeine if we aren't in the mood. We also enjoy the hot guys, and if we stay long enough, we are sure to see at least some of our other friends there.

Bongo Java has a nice front porch. Once again, it is not easy to find parking, but it isn't as cramped as the area around Café Coco. Somehow I can always find a spot on Belmont Boulevard that's not too hard to get into. Bongo Java is also a roasting company, and they have our favorite coffee. They also have great hummus, so it is a win-win situation.

Fido is also a favorite. There is a choice of two or three parking lots, and it is a little easier to get in and out of there. Fido has awesome food, including amazing sweet potato fries, and they serve Bong Java coffee.

One day we found out about a new place called JJ's. Well, the real name is J&J's, but we called it JJ's. It is disguised as a convenience store with a coffee shop in the back. I must have driven down that street a million times and had no idea the treasure that was buried inside. We really like JJ's because it has board games. The only drawback is that smoking is allowed inside, which I can't stand. JJ's is also open later than most of the other coffee shops, which is a big plus. It's too bad we didn't know about JJ's before this one particular night.

It was a beautiful night in mid-July. We had already been to two coffee shops and had closed the Starbucks in Green Hills. It was only ten, and none of us wanted to go home yet. We just wanted to go out and have a good time. We also didn't want to spend any money. We were lamenting that we couldn't all get into a bar, and we didn't want to go to the movies. We'd had enough of the coffee shops and driving around. We weren't sure what to do next.

One of us decided to go up one of the hills where there was an apartment complex and check out the view. Maybe we would get some ideas from looking down at the city. On our way up, we noticed there was a new church, and the church had a playground. The playground had a great view of the city and, *hello*, here was our free activity. We parked the car and got out. There was a chain-link fence around the playground, and the gate had a lock. I knew there had to be a way around it, and I either found it or we climbed over.

We were all having a great time swinging on the swings and running around. We came up with nicknames for ourselves. We were complaining about how there's nothing to do for people under twenty-one. We tried to come up with some solutions, and as always, I complained that Rocketown, the straightedge nightclub owned by my would-be husband Michael W. Smith, had not yet been completed.

Not long after we had arrived, a couple more cars filled with other teens looking for something to do pulled up. They saw us on the playground and noticed the lock on the gate.

"Hey! How did you get in there?" one of them asked.

At first, I pretended not to hear them. If they couldn't figure it out, I wasn't telling them.

Addressing my friends, I said, "What song should we sing next?"

The teens were not happy with my tactics. "Come on! Tell us how you got in. We want to play on the playground, too."

Erica started to tell them how to get in. "If you go around—"

"If they can't figure it out for themselves, then they don't deserve to be here. Besides, they look like trouble."

She realized I was right and got back on the swing.

I knew they were not going to go away quietly. "If you guys can't figure out how to get in, then you can't play on the playground."

I heard them talking to each other. "Come on, guys, let's go."

They quickly left.

The other teens were probably drinking, and I am sure they were underage. I decided we didn't need to be seen with them anyways, and we continued swinging and singing eighties songs.

A little while later, another couple of cars pulled up.

"Not again." I rolled my eyes and tilted my head back. When I was looking forward again I saw that the outline of one of the cars had headlights on the top. "Oh shit. That's a police car! What are we going to do?"

"What did we do wrong?" Zoe asked.

Erica froze.

My brain worked overtime as the policeman and another guy stepped out of their respective cars and slowly walked towards us. "Okay, here's the plan," I said. "We are new to the church, and we just came to play on the playground for a little bit.

There was no time for amendments, so everyone nodded in agreement.

"What are you girls doing?" asked the policeman.

"Oh, we were just swinging," I said.

"Well, you aren't supposed to be here."

"Oh, I didn't realize. We came to the church a few times and decided to come and hang out on the playground for a little while tonight. We didn't know we weren't allowed to play on the playground."

"Were you drinking?" The policeman asked in an accusatory tone.

"No, of course not. We just wanted something to do that didn't involve drinking." I said. The policeman did not believe me. I guess there was just something about me that screamed drunk.

"Well, we got a call saying there were some kids up here drinking in the parking lot."

Zoe stepped in. "There were some other people here a few minutes ago, and they were probably drinking, but we haven't had anything to drink at all tonight."

"Are you sure?"

"Yes."

Then the church guy stepped in. "Now, you girls aren't allowed up here after hours. If you want to come to the services, that's fine. But we can't have you out here after hours because it's dangerous."

"Yeah, I could take you girls down to the station right now for trespassing," the policeman added.

"Um, no. I don't think that's necessary. We won't come back, and we can leave right now. We really just wanted to swing on the swings. That's all, I swear." I prayed they would let us go. If we got arrested because we wanted to be good and not drink, it would not surprise me, but I really did not need a record. If they did take us to the station, I could just hear my parents on the other end of the phone. *You were arrested? For swinging? What?*

The policeman looked at the church guy. "Well, do you want me to press charges? I can take them down to the station right now if you want."

The church guy sighed and turned to us. "Do you promise you won't come back here again? I mean you are allowed to visit the church if you want, but you can't come back to the playground."

"Yeah, we promise," we said in unison.

"Okay then. I guess I won't need to press charges."

We went out our secret entrance to the playground and went back to my car with our hearts pounding. They waited while we drove off.

"Damn! How does this stuff always happen to us?" I asked. "We weren't even drinking! All we were doing was swinging, for God's sake!"

"I know," Erica said. "We could have been doing so much worse. We were just trying to have a good time."

Zoe had been quiet for a few minutes and then said, "It

was those kids who wanted to come in but we wouldn't tell them how. They probably called the police."

"Really? Geez. All they had to do was figure it out for themselves. It wasn't that difficult. I hate people," I said. "Once again, why isn't there anything out there for us to do after the mall closes? We don't need much."

## PTSD911
*Fall 2001*

My heart still skips a beat when I hear a plane overhead. It does not matter where I am; I am never prepared for that sound. I will never forget that day. The phone was ringing, and I hopped down the ladder of my loft bed to answer. I was supposed to be up and out at the mall at the bottom of the World Trade Center to get some school supplies before heading to class.

The call was for my roommate. I gave her the phone and ran to jump in the shower. Before I could get undressed, my roommate yelled for me. I ran to find out what she needed, and she told me the words that changed my life. "A plane hit the World Trade Center." I ran to the window, and instead of the towers, I saw huge clouds of smoke. We immediately turned on the TV to find out what was happening not even a mile away in Manhattan. We went back and forth from the window to the TV until we lost the station. My college was only a few blocks from the towers. I wasn't sure if I should go to school or not. All I could do was stand at the window and stare. My cell phone rang, bringing me back to consciousness. It was the last call that would go through for days.

"I just heard on the intercom at school that a plane hit the World Trade Center," my mom said.

"Yeah I know. My roommate's dad just called and told us."

"Are you okay?" she asked. I later learned that she had no idea how close I was or that my school was right next door. She wanted to make sure I was safe, though.

"I am fine but I don't know what to do. I am supposed to go to class, and our teacher told us we couldn't miss any classes for any reason. But I am afraid to go to Manhattan. I don't think I could get there anyway. I don't think the trains are running. But I don't want to get in trouble or fail this class. I just don't know what to do."

"You should stay where you are. Don't go into the city."

I still felt frustrated about the possibility of letting my teacher down, but it did not seem safe out there—especially since my school was so close. "I'll probably stay here."

We were both in shock but calm. "I'm okay," I told her and myself at the same time. "I should go so we can free up the phone lines."

"Okay. Bye. I love you."

"I love you, too." I had no idea I wouldn't be able to talk to her again for days.

My roommates and I went downstairs to talk to the lady who ran our student housing building. She had been watching from the street when the second plane hit. I saw a trickle of people coming from the Brooklyn Bridge to stand on the entrance of the Brooklyn Queens Expressway to hitch rides. I decided it was not safe to go to school. All transportation had been shut down. Soon the Brooklyn Bridge was packed full of people escaping to Brooklyn. The people walked past my apartment quietly in a daze. Clouds of smoke filled the streets and went right over my apartment building in a steady, thick, toxic stream. We lived next to a fire and police station. The workers at that station were some of the first responders. It was incredibly quiet next door. There were no sirens. No lifting and closing of the gates to get the trucks out. No firefighters chatting outside and smoking. The gates were left open, and no one was there. Later in the day, the trucks started to come back and clean off. The trucks and the firefighters were covered in gray ash, and as they washed everything off, the trail of gray water ran down the sidewalk to my building. At some point, a World Trade Center Security vehicle ended up parked outside. It sat there for a while looking misplaced. I wondered who drove it. I wondered if the driver was okay. The keys were left in the seat. My horrible roommate stole the keys. She saw them sitting there and said, "I'm taking these."

"Why would you do that?" I asked.

"Because I can."

I knew right then she was not the person I thought she was.

I will never forget those images from that day or the days that followed. The smoke filled the sky over my building. The stream of watery gray ash flooded the gutters.

My roommates and I were not sure what to do. One of the four of us was in Manhattan, and we could not get ahold of her. We did not know what happened to her for hours. After sitting around and trying to make sense of what was happening all day, we decided we needed to do something. We had to get out of the apartment and see what we could do to help. We went to the hospital nearby to see if they needed blood. We walked quietly down Flatbush, taking into account the still-steady stream of people around us. Their faces were blank. Some people were crying. Some people were dirty. No one looked back. They just kept walking forward. I wondered how far some of these people had come. How far they still had to go. *Do they have anywhere to go?* We got to the busy hospital and asked if they needed blood, but they didn't at the time. We got lost in the housing projects on our way back to the apartment. But we were not scared. We quietly contemplated our next move. We did not know what was going on because we did not have any cell service or television to tell us what was happening. But the state of the people around us told us all we needed to know. I don't think we ate the whole day.

My school was in Lower Manhattan. Somehow we got the information that all of Lower Manhattan from Canal

Street and below was completely shut down. My school was closed for three weeks since it was located on Chambers Street, and the new building was right next to Building 7 of the World Trade Center. The new school building, Fiterman Hall, had been opened only a few weeks before for the start of the fall semester. It was not quite finished yet. They had not even installed all the carpet. When Building 7 fell, it took the backside of Fiterman Hall with it.

That Thursday, my roommates and I walked to Brooklyn Heights to survey the damage from the Promenade. The sun was setting, and the orange skyline was tinged with smoke. It looked so strange without the towers standing tall and proud. We could not believe the sight of it. The skyline would not change again until after I left New York nine years later. It still confuses me every time I see it.

I had a new friend who lived on Long Island. It was her birthday that Saturday after the attacks, and she invited me to come spend the weekend with her and her family. Since the airports were shut down, I could not go home to Nashville, and I was nervous about being so close to the fires and the toxins the firefighters washed off the fire trucks. My friend's invitation offered me the chance to get out of the toxic air and the depressing environment. So I took the train to Long Island to escape for a few days. It was so nice to be free from the city. I did not have to worry, and even though it was hard to sleep, the peace and quiet let me get some nightmare-free shut-eye.

The airports opened a week later, and I went home for a week. I was scared to get on a plane, but I would have done whatever was necessary to get to the safety of the South. While I was home, I thought about my neighbors, the firefighters. We had been visiting them, bringing them food, and trying to cheer them up. I wanted to do something for them—something to thank them. My mom was an elementary school music teacher, and I was helping her at school in order to get my mind off the tragedy I had witnessed. I decided that the kids could do something for the firefighters. So I got a large white sheet and had every child in the school and all the teachers and aids sign the sheet to thank them for their service. When I returned to Brooklyn the next week, I went to the station and delivered the sheet with all the signatures. They were in shock that an elementary school so far away was so grateful to them for risking their lives to save others and for searching through the rubble and cleaning up the mess. The firemen were very touched that others were thinking of them and that even little kids who could barely sign their names were thankful for their service. They hung the sheet on the back wall of the fire station to remember whom they were fighting for.

Once my school finally opened again, I had to take the train to Chinatown and walk down West Broadway, since the closest subway stations had been destroyed. I still remember the first time I passed the post office in Chinatown. The walls outside were covered in pictures of missing people with names and contact information in case they were found. Little kids had posted drawings of their lost or dead parents. It was a sea of paper.

Those months after, I walked around TriBeCa in a daze, the pit still on fire. The fire had a sharp smell with all the gasoline and metal. I had no choice but to breathe in the ash—tiny pieces of building, people, files, computers. Who even knew at that point what was going into my lungs? Those people, those things, were now a part of me. I still carry them with me.

The sidewalks in lower Manhattan changed color from the ash. No amount of cleaning or repaving kept them black. They kept turning gray again. The Chambers Street ACE subway station was not rebuilt right away. It had a tunnel from Chambers Street to the underground entrance to the World Trade Center. I had used the tunnel all the time my freshman year of school. Even after it had been rebuilt, many years passed before I could walk through that tunnel again without having a panic attack.

I moved across the street from the World Trade Center site three months later. My new apartment complex had been damaged in the attacks. The building across from mine had been hit with plane parts and had not yet been re-opened. My new roommate and I wondered if the people that had been living in our apartment had died. There was no train service close to our apartment for a very long time, so I had to do a lot of walking until the bus routes were re-established. I passed by a parking garage every day, and we could tell that people who had died had left many cars there. Those cars were covered in ash and hadn't moved.

My new apartment was still only a mile from school, but it was now a mile I could walk without having to cross the windy, freezing Brooklyn Bridge. I walked along the Hudson River every day. I couldn't look at the pit where the towers once stood, but I felt it. I felt that I needed to walk past it every day. It was like going to the grave of a loved one every day after he or she had died. I was pretty traumatized from the whole experience. I needed to face the facts constantly to get to the point of finally accepting what had happened. So many people had been upset for a few days, a few months, and then moved on. But I was faced with this tragedy on a daily basis.

After about a year of walking past the pit, this giant hole in the island, I came to accept what had happened and was able to live my life again. The pit had finally been cleaned out of debris, and the repairs had begun. The constant sounds of construction bounced off the buildings and into my apartment. The sound was not always loud, and after a while I got used to it—the constant rhythm reminded me of the beating of a heart. Despite the hate and destruction, we were being reborn. We, as a city and a country, were coming together—making new connections and finding new ways to live our lives for those who could not.

I remember the first anniversary. The news trucks started lining up a week before. They were all decked out with satellites and their news bureau logos. Then the lights. They shot up in the air, taking the place of the fallen towers. At first, they were beautiful, but every year after, I couldn't look at them. From my apartment, I could hear the reading of the names of the people who had died. I tried to stay asleep as long as possible, wanting to forget what I remembered, but the bagpipes woke me up. Mayor Bloomberg's somber voice penetrated the pillow over my head and made me get up and get moving—at the very least for those who could not.

## MAYBE NEW YORK IS NOT FOR ME
### Fall 2001

I was not looking forward to going back to the city after my summer break from college. I felt overwhelming dread as the day came closer. Normally I would already be dreaming of the restaurants I would visit and making a list of Broadway shows I wanted to see. I'd be looking forward to walking everywhere again, too. Instead, I put off packing for the fall semester until the morning I left.

When I got to New York and walked along the sparkly sidewalk on Broadway, the feeling of dread did not disappear. The apprehension became worse. I accidentally left one of my suitcases at the airport, and it took me three hours to realize it. I could not make myself get on the Long Island Rail Road to go back to the airport to retrieve it. The airline sent it to me the next day. I was staying with my previous roommate for a week, since I could not get into my apartment before the first of the month.

I had been in the city for an uneasy week when I finally moved into my own apartment. I had lived in the same student housing loft building for two years on the top two floors. My new apartment was on the second floor. As I walked in the door, the sounds of downtown Brooklyn assaulted me. All the windows were open. I was deafened by horns honking, breaks squeaking, and a siren blaring right outside the window. It had been peaceful and quiet the years before. Now right outside my window was the entrance/exit from the Brooklyn Bridge, the entrance to the Brooklyn

Queens Expressway, a police station, and a fire station. It was so loud. This apartment would be where my insomnia started.

The room was painted a robin's egg-blue color. The set up was different than in years prior. Usually the corner apartments held two Ikea loft beds with a large desk underneath and a huge armoire, just big enough for a college student's wardrobe. Then there was a private room with the same set up, with the addition of a door. This time around, the furniture was smaller, and instead of only two set ups in the main room, the apartment held three. Instead of sleek metal, the furniture sets were made of dark-stained wood. The loft beds were a few feet shorter in height and length, making the desk much smaller, and on the end of the bed, stood a tiny armoire that was maybe two feet square. I could not fit a semester's worth of clothes in there. There were zero shelves for my schoolbooks, but we'd had plenty of shelving and storage in the past. I couldn't put my finger on what was so odd about the furniture, and then I realized it was all children's furniture—children's furniture for college students. Despite the addition of an extra roommate, rent had not gone down at all. I found out later that the private student housing development had sold the top five floors to a school in Brooklyn, so they were trying to make extra money by cramming an extra student into every room on the second and third floors.

I had stashed everything I owned in the storage building next door. I went over there to collect my things. I knew something was off when I walked into my space. It smelled funny, like a musty, old attic with a leak. I had only rented the space for three months. It shouldn't smell bad. Then I saw that the boxes at the bottom of the stacks were wet. I opened them, and the stench of mold became stronger. I opened more boxes. More mold. My sheets, comforter, pillows, clothes—almost all of my things were wet and moldy. The Doc Martens, I had purchased two years before to get me through my first serious winters were green and puffy, the leather completely taken over by the mold. I started to cry.

Apparently, the storage unit had flooded over the summer, but the manager never called to tell me. I had not bought insurance because my stuff was only going to be there for three months, and I couldn't afford the extra cost. I was shit out of luck.

I went back to my still-empty room to cry. I did not even have sheets or a blanket, so I had to borrow those items. I would go back to storage the next day and figure out what to do. Completely devastated, I called my mom. I couldn't figure out why I was so upset. I knew it was normal to be upset about the situation, but I could not stop crying. I was hysterical. My mom said she would help me replace what couldn't be salvaged. I was still inconsolable, so she decided to fly up from Nashville to help me.

My mom arrived the next day. Unlike with her visits before, her presence did not lift my spirits. We were walking in a circle around the basement of Bed Bath & Beyond after a long day of sorting through my trashed belongings. I couldn't decide on a comforter. Nothing felt right. I was completely depressed. I felt like giving up. I felt like leaving the cart of things I had selected in the middle of the store, getting in a cab, and getting on the next plane to Nashville.

"Why are we doing this?" I asked my mom.

"Doing what?"

"Replacing all this stuff? Why am I in New York? What is the point of me being here?

Maybe I should just go back home." I felt like something so much bigger than me was trying to kick me out. I felt like I no longer had a purpose.

"You don't have to stay here if you don't want to."

"I don't want to leave, but I feel like I am not supposed to be here. I don't know why, but I feel like I should quit school and move back home."

"I support you in whatever you want to do," my mom said.

"Why don't we get this bright yellow comforter? Maybe the color will help cheer you up."

A few days later, we were riding in a cab back to my apartment after another trip to Chelsea to replace things. We passed the World Trade Center, and I remember thinking how strange the two buildings looked from the perspective of the cab: two straight columns, as big on the bottom as they were on the top. I had decided I had to stay. I did not want to quit school just because I was depressed. I could get through this, whatever it was.

About a week later, I was walking down West Broadway in the early morning from the subway to Fiterman Hall for class. I was still down in the dumps, but the picturesque scene before me brought out a smile. The sun was rising through the skyscrapers of lower Manhattan. The World Trade Center had the reflection of the sun on two of the four visible skins of the catty-corner towers and was completely dark on the other two. It was so beautiful it took my breath away. I wanted to stop and take a picture, but I didn't want to look like a tourist in trendy TriBeCa. Besides, they would always be there. I could take a picture another day. I had no idea it was my last chance. The next morning, they would be gone forever. I would understand what I couldn't put my finger on—why I had been so hysterical. I would understand that I could feel the evil that was soon coming right to my doorstep.

## MARY FUCKING POPPINS
### *Summer 2001*

Ann Reinking's Broadway Theater Project was three weeks of Broadway boot camp—non-stop singing, dancing, acting, rehearsing, and creating. I looked forward to BTP every year more than I looked forward to Christmas. The workshop was full of juxtaposition and extremes. It was held in Tampa at the University of South Florida. The weather was always crazy. The summer rains soaked us after lunch when we were walking back to the theaters from the dorms. If it wasn't raining, it was blazing hot outside and freezing inside. When I packed for my first workshop, I did not factor in the temperature difference. After freezing through the first day in the theaters, I begged my mom to overnight me some warmer clothes. Each year, we had at least one hurricane warning that would keep us holed up in the dorms. We had late nights and early mornings. They told us we could sleep when we were dead. All the dancing and walking between the dorms and theaters created sore muscles and some of the worst blisters. I wore holes through at least two new pairs of jazz shoes each summer. Celebrities showed up. There was always drama. But no matter what, each year I seemed to have the time of my life.

Broadway Theater Project was one of the few places where I felt like I belonged. People there understood my love of Barbra Streisand, and when I spouted off quotes from random musicals, people knew what I was talking about. For once, people appreciated my creativity, and they invited me to develop it. Students and teachers, who were sometimes Tony Award winners, often incorporated my ideas into our shows. BTP involved laughter and tears; we lived off of pure adrenaline. I couldn't believe the opportunities and experiences that were presented to me. It was like Disney World for hardcore theater people. I never knew what was to come around the corner, but I always knew it was going to be amazing.

I went to Broadway Theater Project for the fourth and final time, mostly because I wanted to perform the song I wrote in the student show. We put the student show together during our nonexistent "free time." I wrote a parody of the song "NYC" from "Annie," and changed it to "BTP" to be about Broadway Theater Project and what a special experience it was. I tried to perform it as a musical number the summer before, but it didn't work out because there were not enough people interested to stage it the way I'd wanted.

The last summer I went to BTP, I finally recruited about eight people—enough to put together a cast. They understood the satirical view I wanted to present to the audience of our peers. We collaborated on the staging, choreography, and direction. We put the piece together as a comic review of our time there. We made fun of ourselves and everyone else. We had a hard time not laughing, and we often cracked ourselves up during rehearsals. One of the parents even bought an Annie wig and shipped it overnight for one of the guys to wear to add to the parody effect. We all thought it was going to be great.

The counselors changed the format that year, and we had to audition for a spot in the student show rather than sign up for a slot. A little nervous but full of enthusiasm, we took our places on the stage for our audition when it was our turn. I don't know what it was, but the vibe in the audience was not what I expected as we waited for the pianist to start. It grew worse as the song went on. No one laughed—not even once. I felt like I was going to be sick as I sang. I never liked seeing the audience as I performed. And this time, as I looked out at the sea of onlookers, I sensed that they were uncomfortable rather than entertained. I knew I had to keep going, even though I could feel my cast falling apart around me. Once it was over, the counselor who had shown me I could write and had helped me find my voice, stared at me unblinking and said flatly, "Thank you." I stood stunned for a minute, and we all left the stage bewildered. No one had laughed. I couldn't figure out why no one laughed. It was really funny, and we had a hard time not laughing ourselves.

The next day, the stone-faced counselor informed me we had to cut two whole minutes out of the four-minute piece. I was confused and upset because they'd told me previously that I didn't have to cut it. I wondered why they'd changed their minds so close to the show. Then my entire cast quit. I was devastated. I didn't know what to do, but I had to share this song. I had worked so hard on it, and I was not one to let other people stand in my way of accomplishing what I wanted to do.

Luckily, I had an amazing roommate. She encouraged me to do the song anyway. She helped me cut it down, and we decided I should sing it like a love song because that's what it was. She was right; I had come too far to just forget about it. I had written the song right before BTP the previous summer. I wanted so badly to perform it in the student show that year, but I could not get enough people to join my cast to make it the production number I wanted it to be. I had no idea if I would be back the next summer to try again, but I wanted Ann Reinking to at the very least have the lyrics. I had cried as I handed her the lyrics I had so lovingly penned. I wanted her to know how much the workshop meant to me. I came back for one more year with the goal of singing this song for her once and for all. I had to make it happen.

The next day, I asked every talented singer I could think of if they wanted to do the song with me. I finally found two willing participants, including a cast member who had dropped out days prior. We had two short rehearsals. I restaged the whole thing to make it simple and to shift the focus of the words. We were a little nervous, but I figured it would be fine. It was just the student show after all, and I really just wanted to say thank you to everyone for being a part of such an amazing experience every summer for the past four years.

A few days before the show, I was breaking the rules and walking back to the dorms by myself for lunch. After a rainy morning, the sun was out again and it was beautiful. The sky seemed incredibly bright to my eyes, which had become accustomed to the dark theater. I put on my sunglasses and trekked across the expanse of sandy grass for the second time that day. Every year we had guest artists ranging from Gregory Hines to Stanley Donen. While I was walking, I just happened to wonder if Barbra Streisand or Julie Andrews would ever be guest artists. I don't know why it came to mind. Barbra, I adore, and I love Julie. I figured that Barbra would never put herself in that position since she doesn't really like her fans so much. Julie was a distinct possibility. I mean, I would never see it happen, and that sucked, but wouldn't that be cool? I could almost see the frenzy of excitement surrounding her entry to Theater 2. Sadly, I had almost finished my time at BTP. I filed the thought away and moved on.

The day of the student show had arrived. I was so nervous. There was a lot at stake. I was going to put myself on display in a way I had not before. I had written this myself. I just wanted people to like the song. I normally danced in the student shows because I felt that dancing was my stronger talent, but this time I was singing. For some reason, the BTP powers that be thought I was a better singer than dancer. Having trained about ten or so years longer in dance, I was much more comfortable with my body as my instrument rather than my voice. I could depend on my body—but my voice? Not so much. I didn't feel like I had as much control over it. I could make my body move with my brain and my muscles. I could feel the movement. When I sang, I could do certain things to make sure the right sound came out, but it was more of an, *I'm going to think this and do this and pray the right note comes out.* I was also nervous because of the lack of rehearsal time. I needed extra rehearsal for singing, and I didn't have that opportunity.

We were all wandering around the theater waiting for the show to start. I kept running outside to practice my part. Finally, the time came for the show to begin. I went inside, and people were still milling about. I paced for a little while and realized it was past time for curtain up. I walked by one of the counselors and overheard her whispering on her two-way radio. "As soon as our special guest arrives, we'll start the show!" I wondered who the special guest could be. Now I had a mystery to solve. At least I had something to keep me from worrying about the song.

We didn't have any guests on the calendar for the next few days. I wondered if it was Marilu Henner. Perhaps she was making up for not being able to come the year before. I couldn't figure out the secret, but I knew it was going to be interesting. I was walking up the stairs to take my seat in the audience when Ann Reinking walked in. She just started talking even though everyone was all over the place. She knew her mere presence would command our attention. She was right. The air shifted as she entered. We all froze and looked to the door like someone had blown a dog whistle. "She is an amazing talent but still puts her family first. There's no one like her! Well, enough introduction … Julie Andrews!" The entire theater stopped moving, whispering, and breathing for thirty seconds until Annie moved from the door. Sure enough Julie Andrews walked in. We all held our breaths wondering if she was a mirage until she threw her hands up in the air and said with her British accent, "Hello!"

The entire theater let out a scream, and we all started jumping up and down. "It's Mary Fucking Poppins! It's Mary Fucking Poppins!" Two minutes later, everyone went quiet. Somehow our collective conscious realized that we had to perform. *For. Her.* We had to sing, dance, and act, *For Mary Fucking Poppins!* I had to sing. I had to sing for Julie Andrews.

I had to sing a song I had written—and had rehearsed only twice—for the best singer in the entire universe. And I had to do it in about fifteen minutes, because we were the third group up. *Oh dear God.*

I took a deep breath, knowing I had to keep it under control or I'd screw the whole thing up. Normally, I did not have an issue with stage fright or anxiety. I did know enough about singing to focus on my breath. If I let my nerves get to me, I would have shallow breath and I wouldn't be able to get the pacing right or hit the right notes. I gave myself a silent pep talk. I was going to go out there, I was going to breathe, and it was going to work out just fine.

I took my place in the makeshift wings for the first number. Once the second number began, I went behind the curtains in the rear to the center of the stage. Theater 2 was a black box, and instead of a backstage with lots of space, there were giant floor-to-ceiling curtains that could be adjusted to each show's needs. There was not much space between the wall and the curtain, and I walked slowly, doing my best not to make waves. I was entering from the curtains in the back stage center. I could not see anything without opening the curtains and stepping onstage. When my number began, I was supposed walk out onto the stage as if I were seeing the atmosphere of BTP for the first time, taking it all in on my own. The second number ended. I walked out onto the stage and gazed around with a dreamy look in my eyes, and then I noticed there were people on stage who were not in my number. I was surprised since the stage was supposed to be empty except for me. My eyes widened a little bit. Not missing a beat, I turned, walked behind the curtain, and wondered what had happened. I found out later that the counselors had added another number to the show before mine and had forgotten to tell me. Neil, a teacher and counselor, later said that when I'd walked out on the stage too early, it turned out to be his favorite part of the show.

The stage crashers finally finished their number, and I waited for the applause to die down while I peeked through the break in the curtains to make sure there were no other surprises. Once the audience finished clapping, I made my way out. I thought about my breath and not the singing nanny sitting right in front of me. I took a big breath. "B- T-" I started to sing, and then I heard Annie's unmistakable cackle. She knew what was coming next. She remembered the lyrics I had given her the summer before. "P," I finished. Then the rest of the audience started laughing. I was very confused. I wondered why they were laughing as I continued to sing. "What is it about you? You're big, you're loud, you're tough. B-T-P." More laughter. What was going on? I finished my verses, and Lori came out to sing her part followed by Carrie. Every time one or all of us sang "B-T-P," the audience laughed. And then they started laughing at the verses. I got a little nervous when I was all on my own out there and noticed Julie Andrews was laughing at me and I had a difficult note to sing next. I took a deep breath and focused on that breath, and the note came out just as it should.

I kept singing it like a love song—like I had rehearsed it—and the audience laughed harder with every verse. By the end of the song, they were roaring with laughter, and Annie's voice rang out above them all. I could see her silhouette in the dark, shaking in time with Julie's next to her. We got lots of hooting and applause while we took our bow. I still didn't understand the laughter, but people were singing my song after the show and on the way back to the dorms and in the hallways, which was all I'd ever hoped for. I was happy.

The next morning, we came back to the theater for a Q&A with Mrs. Andrews. We still couldn't believe she was at BTP. At breakfast we were practically pinching each other; she was all we could talk about. We waited anxiously for her arrival. Once she came in and sat down, we started buzzing again. She finally said, "Hello," and we all squealed. It really was her, she really did have a British accent, and she really was there in front of us.

We were all still very nervous, even though she was sitting there telling us stories. We finally relaxed after she told us a particularly interesting story about when she was filming *Mary Poppins* and had to fly in the brand new Disney studios. They almost dropped her, and she christened the studio by using some very serious curse words. She was clearly one of us.

Then she told us a story about when she was on Broadway in *The Boy Friend*. It was her Broadway debut, and for some reason, her part wasn't working. She couldn't get a laugh out of the audience. One day, the director came to her dressing room during intermission. He said, "Julie, you are playing it funny. You have to go out there and play it straight, and then they will laugh." She thought about this for a few minutes and decided to give it a try. She did the entire second half of the show straight and very serious. The audience loved it, and they laughed hysterically. She was a huge hit.

I was hanging onto every word, and when she got to the end of the story, it hit me. The spotlight in my brain turned on as I realized that was exactly what had happened the night before. I'd played it straight, and they thought it was funny. I had tried to play it funny before, and it wasn't. I looked around at the rest of the students. They didn't seem to share my light-bulb moment. I wanted to raise my hand to tell her she had witnessed me learning that lesson the night before and to thank her for the explanation. For once I decided to keep my mouth shut and relish my new knowledge.

Not only did I get the once-in-a-lifetime chance to sing for Mary Fucking Poppins, and sing a song I'd actually written, but she also taught me the greatest comedy lesson ever. Thanks, Mrs. Andrews, you changed my life in that moment. It shaped my humor and created new avenues for me to get into trouble. I am forever grateful.

## GWEN VERDON or WATCH ME BITCHES
*Summer 2000*

I love dancing like biscuits love gravy. I was a teenager when I fell in love with the Fosse technique. The movements are about sensuality, and the way the body moves is instinctual for me. When I first danced the Fosse technique, I felt like I had tapped into some primal part of myself that I never knew existed. The curve and sway of Bob Fosse's choreographic vocabulary and the sometimes flowing, sometimes angular, staccato movements beat the drum of my heart. He did not have time for romance; he seduced the audience instead. He didn't like to do things like other people. In fact, he took an entire dance style and did exactly the opposite to create his own. He had pigeon toes, so ballet was difficult for him. His turned-in feet are the complete opposite of the sacred ballet turn out. But he did not let his natural stance stop him from dancing. I so admired his *screw you, I'll dance the way that fits my body* attitude. He was a rebel who never let the word "no" stop him. It was as if he always had the goal of pushing the limits further than he really wanted to go, only to reach his intended destination in the first place. He was known for going for straight-up sex on stage, and he always pushed the envelope a little further than he had the time before.

When I was in high school, all my friends were obsessed with Leonardo DiCaprio, but once I discovered Bob Fosse, he was my crush. Whenever I found an artist that intrigued me, I learned everything I could about that person. I watched every movie I could get my hands on that Fosse choreographed or danced in. I read books about him and tried to learn more about the dancers who surrounded him. I learned about his wife Gwen Verdon, who was a Broadway diva and Bob Fosse's muse. I couldn't find any books about her, but I noticed that her persona jumped off the screen when she danced. She was the original Lola in *Damn Yankees*. When I saw her performance of "Whatever Lola Wants" I knew I wanted to be her. She had just enough attitude, and she was extremely confident. She knew how to reel in her target with her slow, subtle moves and then hook him with a quick, precise tilt of her hip. I could not decide what I liked best, her performance or Fosse's choreography. Their collaboration was magical.

*Damn Yankees* was the first movie where I saw Bob Fosse dance. He was in "Who's Got the Pain" with Gwen. The way they swiveled and flew across the stage together delighted me. I couldn't help but smile. Besides her dancing abilities, Tony Awards and firecracker ways, Gwen was also short like me. It gave me hope that maybe my short stature would not stand in my way of a career in dancing, a field where midsize height is prized.

Gwen was also the original Roxie Hart in *Chicago*, my favorite Bob Fosse musical. I loved listening to her version of the Roxie monologue while I was driving to dance classes. I loved trying to mimic her delivery. When *Chicago* was revived on Broadway in 1996, I recorded the Tony Awards on my VCR. *Chicago* was nominated for several awards, and I wanted to study and learn the choreography. I was in awe of the dancers, especially Bebe Neuwirth and Ann Reinking. I was impressed with their precise movements. It would take a lot of practice to perfect the choreography, but it was a great way to study the technique and complex movements. With Fosse technique, even your little finger has choreography, and it has to be perfect.

My third summer at Ann Reinking's Broadway Theater Project, Gwen Verdon and Roy Scheider were guest artists. Roy played Bob Fosse in the movie *All That Jazz*. He may be the "We're going to need a bigger boat," guy from *Jaws* to most, but to me he is Fosse. I had seen *All That Jazz* countless times, and Roy was the visual representation of Fosse in my mind. It was like meeting Fosse himself. Even Ann Reinking, Fosse's other muse, said that when they were shooting *All That Jazz*, that if Roy had his back turned, she would have conversations thinking it was Fosse and be startled when Roy turned around. He not only looked like Fosse, with a cigarette carelessly hanging out of the side of his mouth, but he also matched his spunky attitude. I was ecstatic that I had the opportunity to meet them both. It was not something I'd ever expected to happen. I once again counted down the days to BTP.

The day arrived that Gwen came to Broadway Theater Project, and everyone was falling all over each other with more excitement than usual. Broadway Theater Project was three weeks of pure adrenaline, and this was the height of it all. We kept ourselves occupied with constant chatter from the cafeteria to Theater 2 where most of the big action took place. We never really knew what would happen at BTP until the night before. We sometimes had an idea of when guest artists were coming, but no one ever gave us specifics ahead of time. It was probably best because the anticipation alone would have worn us out. When the staff had delivered our schedules the night before, we all speculated about what we'd be able to do with Gwen. Some guest artists only participated in question-and-answer sessions, some also taught one big or small group class, and others worked on special pieces for the show we performed at the end of the three weeks. We were lucky that Gwen was able to do all three. She was going to be with us for an entire week. The thought of getting to dance with her the next afternoon kept me awake a little longer than usual until exhaustion took over.

I could not believe it was really happening when Gwen walked into the dance studio for my group class. Her hair was still fiery red, and her voice quivered with Essential Tremors. She taught us the choreography from part of "Who's Got the

Pain" from *Damn Yankees,* and I could not believe I had the opportunity to see her dance live. Despite being in her seventies, she could still move with sensuality and flair. Her attitude matched her flaming red hair. While she taught us, I could visualize her dancing on screen with Bob. I watched and listened carefully, cataloguing her every movement and word. This was one of the most important moments of my dance career.

We practiced the choreography individually before adding music. I knew I had to get this right. Sometimes I had trouble picking up chorography quickly. For some reason my brain did not always want to cooperate. I was determined to get this combination of eight counts into my body and soul in spite of my brain. I think Gwen knew how badly we wanted to get it right. Aside from the sound of our jazz shoes sliding around and turning on the gray dance floor, everyone was uncharacteristically silent. Gwen went around the studio correcting people and helping them with the movements they didn't understand. I was concentrating on a difficult part of the dance, making sure it was perfect. As she corrected other students, I listened, and used those corrections to improve myself. Suddenly, someone asked a question from across the room.

Gwen said, "Watch her. She's got it."

I turned around to watch the girl who was doing it right. I realized all eyes were on me. My eyes widened. Gwen Verdon was using me as an example. I knew I was a good dancer, but rarely did an instructor call me out for my talents unless I was on the floor alone—especially at Broadway Theater Project. Everyone stared at me and waited for me to demonstrate the choreography, so I shakily began moving. This was my moment. I would not be like Roxie Hart and let opportunity pass me by. I worked with as much determination and precision as I could muster. My brain sent rapid-fire messages to my body: *roll hips, move index finger, turn in legs.* As I danced, Gwen explained my technique. I could not believe that my favorite living dancer was telling everyone I was doing it right.

I wish I could remember what she said, but I was focusing so intensely on my movements that the words were lost as soon as they escaped her mouth. All those years of practicing *All That Jazz* in living rooms across Tennessee had not been in vain. The expert on Fosse technique had picked me as an example. I was astonished. I wished all those teachers and students who had looked down on me, who had told me no, or who had just plain overlooked me could have been in that room at that moment. I thought, *If my friends could see me now, I would say to them, "She said to watch me, bitches. I am doing it right. Follow me. Watch my technique. I've got it."*

I knew I was a good dancer. I knew how to take the passion inside my heart and translate it to my hips, shoulders, and eyes. I rarely had the opportunity to express that passion. Most of the professional dance I was involved in was ballet. Unless a dancer has a solo, she is not supposed to shine; instead she should fit in with the group. She should move exactly in time and equally spaced apart from the other dancers. I was often a part of a specific scene in *The Nutcracker*, where there was some individualism, but that was more acting and involved less complicated choreography.

In my teen years, I had devoted most of my studio dance time to ballet classes, but I longed for my turn to seduce the audience with my Fosse ways. Not many jazz teachers in Nashville taught his technique. I was fortunate enough to take some jazz classes with a teacher who knew Fosse technique, but I craved more. I always looked forward to the requisite Fosse classes at Broadway Theater Project. Aside from the few Fosse-focused classes I'd had in Nashville, I'd mostly taught myself the intricacies of his style.

I loved working up a sweat with my efforts to perfect the synchronistic curve of the arms and the hips, the roll of the joints side-to-side, and the forward Fosse walk, which was the foundation of his technique. Even though I loved dancing on my own, when I practiced, I craved an audience to feed off of. I wanted eyes in front of me to stare down as I Fosse-walked that fine straight line forward. I wanted someone to be enthralled with my perfection like I was enthralled with Ann, Bebe, and Gwen. I loved ballet and longed for a chance to perform the parts on stage that would allow me to show my passion for dance, but it was not in the cards for me. After an injury, lack of growth in the vertical direction, and a change of heart, I realized my curves were not meant for tutus. My hips were made to swivel with Fosse. I wanted so badly to make my living dancing and singing in Fosse musicals on Broadway. Even with all my hours of dancing and training, I never made the cut from the fierce competition into the Fosse numbers that were always a part of our final show. But right there, in Studio B, Gwen Verdon picked me. She picked me, and I will never forget it.

Watch me, bitches.

# TRANSITIONS
## *Summer 1999*

The transition from idea to execution is the process of creation. The creation often needs a transition to tie it all together. Sometimes the hardest part of creating is the transition. But when you get it right, the transition can be magical.

I went to Ann Reinking's Broadway Theater Project for four summers in a row. It was like Broadway boot camp—singing, dancing, and acting all day every day for three weeks straight. At the end of the three weeks, we did a show at the Tampa Bay Performing Arts Center. Teachers and guest artists put it together. We did all sorts of numbers, musicals, dances, and scenes from a wide variety of shows that had been on Broadway or were born onto Broadway after being "workshopped" on the students.

Ann Reinking is a protégé of Bob Fosse. She performed in some shows with him, choreographed the revival of *Chicago,* and starred as Roxie Hart. After we had learned and rehearsed our numbers, she started to weave the show together like a technicolor dream coat. She would watch us all perform, and right away, start to find the order and put the pieces in their places. She would find a way to make one number transition to the next for one seamless show. I loved watching her perform her magic. She had a lot of different transitions, some as simple as one group bleeding into the next as one left and the other entered. Others were more complicated and took about half an hour to finally execute.

She would pick a person and start to have them speak or move. Sometimes I doubted her choice. I could see the wheels were turning, but I couldn't see where they were going. I knew it was going to be interesting when she left her perch in the audience to get closer to the action. She would talk to the people she was transitioning and give them direction, sometimes choreography. At times I thought she had gone too far, that her idea wouldn't come across. But I was always wrong. Somehow, she pulled the most random ideas out of the air and made it seem like the most natural thing on earth.

I always tried to sit close to her during the transition rehearsals so that maybe some of her genius would somehow transfer to me. I wanted to overhear her reasoning as she talked to her partner and they smoothed out the details. What would she come up with this year? How would she combine Burt Bacharach, Burns and Allen, and a contemporary piece some of us had written and choreographed? Sometimes I wish I had her around to make my transitions in life go more smoothly. Life would be much more magical with Annie to wave her hands around and make the pieces fall into place.

I would ask her to cast someone for me to spend the rest of my life with. That way I wouldn't have to blindly stumble around the dating world. She would gloss over the messy parts of life after I'd experienced a serious illness. She would help me stretch through the tightness of my tired and frustrated days. She would make the most of my dark moments and help me to fly across the stage in the spotlight. She would help me make the most of my life, and I would love having her around.

Now that my time at BTP is over, I miss Annie. I remember watching her sit in her various spots in the front row of Theater 2 with her plastic bag of makeup. I marveled at her bullet-shaped lipstick. How very Roxie Hart of her. I was right there with her when she performed the Roxie Hart monologue for us, and I finally understood some of the nuanced references. I focused on the choreography of each and every finger. I admired the way she slightly turned her head but still looked at us out of the corner of her eye. Even her eyes had chorography. Every step and gesture had a meaning, and it delighted my heart.

The first time I saw her, I thought I might have a heart attack. I was so anxious and nervous. *What if she didn't like my dancing? What if I couldn't move my hips just the way she wanted? What if I couldn't make her laugh?* What if she didn't notice me at all? It was my first night at Broadway Theater Project. We were all in an empty room at the dorm's cafeteria. I caught a glimpse of her while we were all filing in for orientation, and it startled me. All of a sudden, the gravity of the situation dawned on me. I was on the verge of the workshop I had been waiting so long for. So many opportunities lay before me. I would be able to work with some important people. There were so many creative possibilities. I had been increasingly nervous all week. Now Ann Reinking was sitting only a few feet in front of me. It was happening. I silently shook in the freezing Florida air conditioning, watching her as I halfway listened to the counselors give us the rundown on what we had gotten ourselves into. I couldn't wait for Annie to speak. I wanted to hear everything she had to say.

As the workshop began, I found myself fascinated with her. I was astounded watching her work. It was as if her creativity knew no bounds—except for when it came to her clothes. She always wore the same outfit, a slinky long-sleeved black sweater with a white-collared button down underneath and tight black pants. There was a hilarious thread of emails going around to the BTP students one summer about her one outfit. She even wore that same outfit to the Tony Awards instead of a fancy dress. Then she wore it again on Regis and Kelly. I imagine she had too much transitioning to do to bother with costume changes.

Before I met Annie, I watched her over and over on the Tony Awards with Bebe Neuwirth when they were nominated for *Chicago*. They danced the "Hot Honey Rag," and I dragged my tape around with me everywhere, practicing it—just in case there was an opportunity to dance it with her. Oh, how I would have died over that. I went over and over the footwork, trying to get it just right. I knew how obsessed she was with detail, and I wanted to impress her if the opportunity arose.

Her schedule dictated her presence at the project. Some years, the students were lucky to have her there at all. One summer, we pretty much had her to ourselves the entire three weeks. We kept expecting her to disappear, but she showed up every day. We were a tight ship that year. She learned more about us from teaching and watching. It bled into the show. We all felt so connected to her that summer. It was like we were one big family.

I always wanted to be in a piece for our final show with Annie. As hard as I worked on Fosse technique, there were at least fifty other girls who could Fosse-walk me into a corner. Because of her tight schedule, some years she only worked on the Fosse numbers for our final show—and nothing else. I always looked at the casting board with hope that the teachers would notice me and cast me in a number with her. Then one day it happened. I was in the crowd of people after dinner in the halls of the theater building, checking out the notice board to see where I had to go that evening. I was scanning the names and found myself listed on the show she was directing. I had to read it three times to make sure my eyes were not playing tricks on me. I was incredibly lucky to be in a group that had the opportunity to collaborate on a new piece with her.

I was nervous as I walked into Theater 1. The number was to the theme song to *Austin Powers*, and it was a big group. I could tell she was having so much fun with the piece once we got started. Some of the pressure melted away, and I had fun too. There was no pressure for her to please Tony and Drama Desk voters. Even though this piece was going into the final show, it was pure fun. She did not have to do it herself. We all worked together. I don't think she yelled at us once during that rehearsal period. We were welcome to add our ideas and input. There was even a moment where I had an idea but kept it to myself, and two seconds later, Annie was implementing that exact idea into the piece. I loved the opportunity to be on the same wavelength with her.

Annie was hilarious, and some days she kept us laughing until we cried. She also had a super-serious side, and her lectures could leave us terrified. Making Annie mad was not something anyone wanted to do, but it did happen every now and then. The older students always warned the new kids to stay in line when she was there. We had much more fun when she was teaching, choreographing, and directing us. Her lectures were legendary. Definitely, at times, our behavior warranted some yelling. The long days were exhausting, and toward the end of the three weeks, we could get loopy during rehearsals. She had no patience for goofing off. She could be very sweet, but it only took one raise of her voice, and we were stunned into submission.

Even though she could be scary, all the students adored Annie. She inspired us to commit to every single little thing we did. She told us to avoid mediocrity. She would say, "If you are going to make a mistake, make it big. Make a mistake because you are committed to what you are doing." Her words have stuck with me ever since. She inspired us to keep going despite rejection. She inspired us by saying, "Sometimes people create their own theater out of imperfection." I am a perfectionist, but I found that there is just as much art in the imperfection. I am not as afraid of imperfection anymore.

The day I gave her the lyrics I had so lovingly written about BTP, I cried. She cried. I had grown to love her. She was my idol, and I just wanted to follow her around and watch her work. I was so sad when I finally had to say goodbye after my last summer at BTP. My time at the project was over, and I never wanted it to end.

Please, Annie, come back and choreograph my life. I'll love you forever.

## MISO DEAD
### *Fall 2000*

I went home to Nashville the weekend before Thanksgiving to see my friend Marilu Henner in the Broadway tour of *Annie Get Your Gun* at the Tennessee Performing Arts Center. I was getting together with a big group of friends to see the show and then have dinner with her between the matinée and evening performance. I was really nervous about the food because of my multitude of food allergies. We were eating across the street from the theater at the Hermitage Hotel. I had sent my laundry list of allergies to the person who was organizing the event, but I just couldn't get the butterflies out of my stomach.

I dislike having to dine out when the courses are from a pre-set menu. I hate events where everyone eats the same thing because that never works out for me. Usually the food is made ahead of time, and there is usually some offending item in every single dish. Then I am left with a piece of bread, if that, and have to explain the allergy thing to the whole table. It's embarrassing, and I am so over all those questions.

Food was very rarely exciting for me at that time in my life. I knew the menu would be dairy and meat free, but I wasn't convinced the meal would be safe for me. The servers gave us a menu, so we knew what to expect with each course. The first course, miso soup, stirred up the butterflies. First of all, I was not into soup at the time. Soup is sneaky. It might look safe, but often times there's a hidden ingredient I am allergic to. I run the risk of eating something that might make me sick. Second, miso is normally made with rice. There are varieties of miso that are made with other things like barley or chickpeas instead of rice. At the time, I was severely allergic to rice. I didn't get the impression that the chef would realize that miso is made with rice and that it could make me sick.

We were seated at a long rectangular table. I was sitting on Marilu's side with one person between us and across from Tammy, who'd organized everything. My friend Ali was sitting next to me, and Marilu was on her other side. Ali was telling us a captivating story as the servers brought out the soup. I caught a glimpse of it across the table and could tell by the light yellow color it was most likely the miso made with rice.

I took a deep breath. The server placed my soup in front of me. I wanted to ask about the miso, but I couldn't without drawing attention to myself and away from Ali. The server disappeared quickly anyway. I decided I would just let it sit there and hoped no one would notice I wasn't eating. A few minutes later, Tammy noticed I wasn't slurping away like everyone else. She mouthed across the table, "No rice. It doesn't have any rice in it." I thought it would be impolite if I didn't try it. The last thing I wanted was for her to think I was rude. I didn't even remember the last time I'd had rice. Maybe the reaction wouldn't be so bad. My hand shook as I picked up my spoon and dipped it into the soup. I lifted it to my lips and took the smallest possible sip. Maybe if I took forever to eat it, the next course would come and the server would take it away before I had the opportunity to finish. I decided this was the only way to do it.

I was still alive. I took another deep breath and dipped the spoon back into the soup. I brought it to my lips and took a small sip. I tried to swallow. I couldn't. My throat was tight. I tried again. Nothing. My tongue seemed to take up my whole mouth. Something was wrong. I tried swallowing again. I started to choke. I slid down in my chair as I continued to choke. *Oh, God. I am dying. God, if you are ready to take me, I am ready to go.* I was having trouble being quiet. I didn't want to interrupt Ali's story, and if I was going to die, I wanted to go quietly and politely. I slid down a little more. As hard as I tried, I couldn't be quiet. *Oh, God, what am I going to do?*

Marilu was facing me as Ali told her story. She noticed something was going on and asked if I was okay. I shook my head no.

"Are you choking?" I shook my head yes. Ali turned around and beat me on my back as hard as she could. I am not sure how, but it worked, and I started to regain my breath. I didn't pick up my spoon again. I didn't want to die. I wanted to see Marilu perform onstage, finally. Then I could die.

The rest of the dinner went by without any drama. Caffeine sometimes slows allergic reactions, so I had coffee after the dinner. The coffee helped me to resume my evening, so I did not have to skip the show that I so badly wanted to see. I found out later that the miso was made with rice. The chef had no idea there were multiple varieties of miso. Tammy was very apologetic, and I was mortified. It was not her fault. I had almost died in front of Marilu Henner and about fifteen other people.

## NASHVILLE BALLET AND STRESS FRACTURE
### Fall 1994

Nashville Ballet was like my high school. I had to homeschool to be able to perform in *The Nutcracker* with them and any other shows. The ballet was the place I spent most of my time. It was my pain and pleasure. The ballet was my source of elation and deep depression. I worked harder than anyone else in my level. If I had to miss a class due to rehearsal or a show, I took another class at a lower level and made up my absence, which was required. Most people just missed classes and didn't care about making them up. Somehow they slipped through the cracks and avoided punishment. But I was dedicated and viewed taking class at a lower level as an opportunity to brush up on my technique.

Each level had to wear a certain color leotard along with pink tights. It was our uniform. It helped the people in charge categorize us. The expectations were different for the light blue group than for the royal blue or burgundy students. We had to watch out for the light blue leotards. That level was like the doldrums in the sea. If we were not careful, we could get stuck there and remain stagnant for years. I had classes and sometimes rehearsals six to seven days a week. My teachers used to correct me a lot; other times they completely ignored me. There was not much middle ground. One teacher loved to yell across the room and over the loud piano: "Breathe, Heather!" I would focus so much on the placement of my body that I would forget about my respiration.

Just like with everything else, I had my weird talents. I was incredibly flexible and was often called Gumby. I could do a giant *grande sissonne ouverte*, basically a big open jump, lifting the front leg forward and kicking the back leg up, like opening scissors all the way. As I jumped, my back leg had so much mobility I could kick the bun on my head with my leg. I could do the splits in a doorframe with my legs on the one side of the frame and walk my hands up the other side. I'd be almost standing up straight with my legs still in the splits along the doorframe behind me. My back was so flexible, I could do back handsprings, and my hands would land in the same spot where my feet had been, and then my feet would return to the same spot, as well. I was also really good at falling. I didn't realize it at the time, but I had vertigo, so too much spinning around left me on the ground, even though I used my eyes to stare at a spot on the wall and whip my head around as I turned. The worth of a dancer is often found in how many turns he or she can do at one time. I eventually found my center, which is different for each dancer, and it helped turns become effortless. I could feel it deep in my stomach like a compass near a magnet. If I could connect to it, my turns just happened just because. Then there were the days that no matter how hard I tried, I could not find it, and I would fall a time or two. I had a handle on falling, though. Falling is not allowed in ballet, but if you do fall, you are supposed to get up and keep dancing. Some people would fall on the floor during class and just stay there. Not me. I rolled out of it in time with the music and got right back up without missing a beat. I even got a standing ovation during rehearsal once for my ability to fall on my ass and make it look pretty—like it was part of the choreography.

I was very serious about my dance training. All I wanted to do was dance all day. And some days, that's all I did. I would get ready for class in the afternoon by putting my make-up on, brushing my hair, and winding my hip-length locks into the tiniest bun. Then I'd add half a bottle of hairspray or gel to smooth back the inevitable flyaways. Next,

I'd work on my stretching and a floor barre routine—the same routine every day. I'd start at two at one dance studio with a ballet class and then go straight to jazz and then tap. I had half an hour to drive across town, which was just enough time to make it to my next ballet class at Nashville Ballet and then a pointe class—ending the day with a total of six or more hours of dancing. I would go home, eat dinner, collapse into bed, and start again the next day with different classes and a different schedule. It was hard work, but I loved it. Without dance, my life was incomplete. My dad used to shoo me out of the kitchen when he was cooking dinner because I tap danced so much I made the house shake. I could see my feet moving in the reflection of the glass cover of the oven. And the parquet floor was the only place suitable to tap. He made me watch *You Can't Take it With You* because the daughter in the movie danced all the time, especially in the kitchen, and I reminded him of this character.

I worked so hard, through sore muscles and exhaustion. The hours spent in pointe shoes resulted in painful blisters. Many days I was so sore I couldn't walk up or down the stairs. I had to sit and scoot down the steps on my butt or crawl up them on all fours. Despite all the pain, dancing was what freed my soul.

It didn't just hurt physically; it sometimes hurt emotionally, as well. Ballet is heartless when it comes to the politics involved in casting parts for the productions or selecting dancers for the advertisements. Even the little things like deciding who will give out flowers to the principal dancers on opening night involve politics. As much as it hurt, I loved it. Despite the median retirement age of thirty-five to forty for a dancer—if you don't get injured before that—I had plans to spend the rest of my life on my toes. I would find a way.

I started to have back problems around age fourteen. I did not realize it at the time, but my left hip had been dislocated during birth, and the doctors put it back in slightly the wrong place. I now realize this caused a number of alignment issues and problems with muscles all along my left side. I went to the chiropractor and found I had slight scoliosis and that the bone above my tailbone was pushed slightly forward. We couldn't afford continued visits to the chiropractor. One of my ballet teachers was getting certified in Pilates and started teaching us little bits of it during class. It was healing movement focused on correcting imbalances in the body. Dancers take technique class daily to help balance out their bodies. During rehearsals, dancers practice choreography for upcoming shows. Most of the time, the choreography is not balanced. A movement might be performed on one side of the body but not the other. This causes imbalance in the muscles, which can lead to injury. This is one of the reasons Pilates is so important for dancers. Pilates was helpful for me, but my back still hurt.

When I was seventeen, my sciatic nerve, which is located in the hips where the pelvis meets the sacrum at the end of the spine, became a problem. Pain would shoot down the back of my leg after class. Then it started to hurt during class, and after a while, it would hurt so bad it would temporarily paralyze me while I was dancing. I didn't want to stop dancing no matter how much it hurt, so I would just keep going. We would be practicing our recital piece in class. Everyone would be moving, and then I would just stop, frozen in whatever pose had caused the pain. I was temporarily paralyzed. As much as I wanted to keep moving, my body would not let me. My teacher made me sit out when I couldn't move, and she encouraged me to go see a doctor.

I knew my body so well. It wasn't my muscles. It was my nerve, and after a while, the bones in my spine began to hurt. The general practitioner tried to tell me it was my muscles and gave me muscle relaxers, but I knew better. After a couple of weeks with no improvement, I had to go see the orthopedist. I was scared he would tell me I had to stop dancing. I did not know what life would be like without dance. I had been dancing as long as I could remember.

I was almost eighteen. It was the spring of my senior year. I was so excited to finally be going to New York in the fall where I could take dance classes any day of the week as often as I could afford it. I wanted to be in a ballet company for a few years after college with the ultimate goal of dancing on Broadway. All I thought about everyday was getting to New York and dancing my heart out. Not dancing was not an option.

The orthopedist was very nice. He took care of the Nashville hockey team, the Predators. Because of that, I felt like he would understand how important my dancing career was to me. When he came back with my X-rays, I tried not to cry. My spine was a mess. I could see through some of the bones. My vertebrae had white outlines and black holes in the middle of the bones. My bones looked fragile and weak. The view from the front of my body showed that my spine was unnaturally curved to the left side, and my slight scoliosis had progressed to mild. My spine was all out of whack. It looked like someone had taken a wire hanger and mangled it. He said I had a stress fracture in my lower back. It is a common injury for young dancers. He hesitated and took a deep breath as he said the words I feared. "You have to stop dancing." I couldn't hold the tears back any longer, and he handed me the tissues.

"But I can start dancing again later, right?" I asked.

He said we would have to wait a month and check it again to see if it healed at all. He couldn't promise that I would be able to dance again.

After the appointment, I was in shock. I wasn't sure what I would fill my life with instead of dance. Even though I am a planner, I could not think past those moments that were right in front of me. I did the only thing I could think to do: go to the ballet studio. I told the administrators I had to stop dancing due to my injury. There were only about nine weeks left in the semester at ballet and I could not dance for six weeks. There was no guarantee I would be able dance the last three weeks. There was no need to keep paying for dance classes if I could not take them. It was hard, but I saw this as a sign that I didn't need to be there any longer. There had been a lot of issues with some of the teachers and administration lately anyway. As much as I loved dancing, it was no longer a joy to dance there but a literal pain in the ass. I made it through my difficult conversation without too many tears and made my way home never to return.

I walked into the house and turned on the TV, needing to numb and forget. It was on PBS, and of course there were a bunch of skinny girls dancing at Lincoln Center. I knew the music. I knew the choreography to the variation they were doing. I couldn't remember the name. All I could do was stand there staring and wondering what was wrong with them. Why weren't they singing, or talking? Why did they just smile and look pretty? Why didn't they have any emotion behind their pretty faces and perfect bodies? The New York City Ballet was performing *Sleeping Beauty* live from Lincoln Center. My dad was going to tape it for me but forgot. As I stared at the dancers on the screen, a shift started in my brain. Something clicked, and I was forever changed. I realized that the New York City Ballet was just flitting around the stage as if to say, *Look at me; I'm so pretty!* They had absolutely no artistry, no emotion, just *look at how high I can lift my leg* and that was it. If that was what I was expected to aim for, I wanted no part in it. Ballet could suck it.

I still wanted to move and dance, but that was not a guaranteed option. I had just been told not to even bend over and touch my toes. Movement wasn't going to be happening anytime soon. I called my other teachers and dance schools and let them know what was up. I wasn't sure what to do with my life without dance in it. I had danced as long as I could remember. It was a constant. To stop dancing was to stop living. It was so painful that I have blocked that initial dance-free time out of my memory.

After a month, I went back to the doctor. He said my spine looked better and decided I could try dancing again if I didn't overdo it. I had to stay on the pain medication for a while.

I will never forget the first dance class I took after the break. It was a ballet class, and it was like my life before had not been my own. Both the instructor and the owner of the studio ignored me and treated me like they didn't even know me, even though I had been dancing at the studio for five years. I could barely lift my leg behind me. My limbs felt like lead. I couldn't get my body to cooperate. I had to think very hard about how to move my muscles, something that had been second nature only six weeks ago. I had to think about so many things at once. I had no idea how I had done it before. The simplest exercises were now frustrating and difficult. It was like someone had turned the power off in my body. My muscles felt heavy and uncoordinated. A serious injury and a month off had erased the hard work I had been doing all my life. Little did I know that it was much more than a stress fracture I was suffering from.

I did not know how I was going to get back to the way I had danced before. I had classes and rehearsals six to seven days a week. The school semester was over, and my final dance recital was coming up. I also had Broadway Theater Project in a month. I needed to take a lot of classes to get stronger again. I needed to work on my technique and teach my body how to move after six weeks of stagnation. Because the school year was over, there were not enough classes available for me to take to rehab my body. I knew for sure I didn't want to be a ballerina, but I still wanted to dance.

After the painful ballet class ended, I escaped the studio as quickly as I could. I sat in my car overwhelmed by my feelings. I felt insignificant to the people I had looked up to for so long. I felt lost in a sea of ballet terms, forgotten angles, and poor muscle memory. I was angry with my teachers for seeing me as a lost cause. I realized this was probably the end of my dancing career; it hadn't even had a chance to begin.

## THIS HEART
### *Spring 1998*

My favorite ballet of all time is *This Heart*. Paul Vasterling choreographed it for the Nashville Ballet to commemorate the bicentennial of Tennessee. It featured the songs of Nanci Griffith, a folk artist who lives in Nashville. There was something special about *This Heart*. Unlike most traditional story ballets and even contemporary pieces, it was joyful and triumphant. It had an energy all its own. Nanci Griffith has a unique voice that rings like a bell. Her tones are clear and clean. The songs each had their own tone in their small story world. The smallness of Nanci with her band of three—compared to the normal symphony of instruments—also set it apart. The drums stood out when a string section no longer overpowered them. The beat of the music rattled through the walls of studio A as the company rehearsed. The treat of beautiful lyrics after years of instrumental music was a welcome change. It stood apart from the other ballets purely for its exuberant theme. It was magic.

I remember walking up the steps to the ballet studios that we shared with the company. It was the first warm day of spring, and there were three red-faced, sweaty dancers on the stairs. They were bent over gasping for air. They looked completely exhausted but not in the usual way. Something serious was going on inside, and I rushed in to find out what.

I went to the dressing room to get changed and walked out to the makeshift lobby area to stretch and watch the end of rehearsal. The music started, but it wasn't the normal classical, dramatic music. It was folk music, and the dancers didn't seem completely drained as they danced through hour six of rehearsal. I recognized the singer's voice but couldn't place it. One of my friends told me it was Nanci Griffith. The dancers had smiles on their faces, and they seemed to be genuinely happy. What a change from the usual looks of concern they held when the theme was clichéd death and unrequited love.

The song "This Heart" started to play, and everyone in the lobby stopped to watch. It was magnetic. Nanci's happy voice and cheerful guitar spun the dancers around with a joy I had never seen in them before. A small crowd had gathered around Studio A by the end of the song. I felt the urge to get out of my pretzel shape on the floor and give them a standing ovation. Instead, I had to run to class.

Over the next few weeks, *This Heart* had made an impression on everyone who entered the studios. The company members, teachers, students, and parents seemed to be in a better mood. I noticed less yelling and more encouragement in class. I swear I jumped higher, feeling the lift of Nanci's voice in the background. The music played loudly in Studio A while we tried to pay attention to the live piano echoing through the cavernous Studio B. I sat on a bench next to the wall we shared with Studio A. My legs were tired, and I was out of breath from the leap combination I had just completed. I could feel the beat of "This Heart" through the wall, beating my own heart. It reverberated in my ribcage so fiercely that I thought my ribs would break. It gave me the energy and passion I needed to dance the combination across the floor despite the heat and exhaustion that surrounded me.

Between our technique class and variations, we would gather in the lobby to put on our pointe shoes and let the lilt of "Nobody's Angel" calm us down as we watched the company rehearse. Even our normally stern teacher leaned against the doorframe, watching with joy in her tired eyes.

Nanci Griffith transformed our lives during the weeks the company rehearsed the ballet. If they were rehearsing *Giselle* or *Swan Lake* we were our usual bitter selves—complaining about homework, teasing someone about how they fell on their ass in the middle of class, or comparing our bodies in the wall of mirrors until the teacher came in. Instead we were all happy. We forgot about how much our feet hurt or the test we had the next day and just enjoyed dancing instead.

Everyone had a smile on his or her face during *This Heart*. Nanci's harmonies and calming voice soothed our teen hurts and encouraged us to keep dancing for the heck of it. I didn't think it could get any better until I saw the opening night performance. Nanci Griffith and The Blue Moon Orchestra were performing live. My best friend at the time and I had gotten free tickets. We sat in the front row, and it was amazing. The energy poured out of the company as they flit about the stage. It was even more energetic with the addition of lights, audience, and live music. I had never seen the company members so happy to be on stage and dancing. The audience loved it and gave a standing ovation. It was not your typical night at the ballet. After the weekend of performances, we went back to our usual selves. We were all stressed out with the demands of school, dance, and whatever other extra-curricular activities that had been piled on our plates.

The next school year, things went back to normal. The company rehearsed another depressing ballet, and we got ready for *Nutcracker* auditions. That spring, the ballet did *This Heart* again, and the magic that the ballet brought to the studio returned.

A few years later in New York, I would listen to Nanci's album *The Flyer*, with some of the music from *This Heart*, whenever I felt homesick. It would transport me back in time to my happiest memories of home. I could feel the warmth of the studio and hear Nanci's guitar encouraging my aching muscles. I could be sardined on the subway in the early morning, but if I closed my eyes and listened to "This Heart," the whole city melted away. I could see Nanci on the apron of the stage with her gray hair and shining eyes, playing and tapping her foot to the music, as the dancers flew across the theater in their cowboy boots and denim.

I finally met Nanci when I was thirty. It was so nice to be able to thank her in person for turning a stressful, bureaucratic environment into a peaceful, happy one.

## I CAN'T SEE GUYS, I CAN'T SEE
*Winter 1998*

I fell in love with acting when I was in elementary school. I was in a school play in third grade. I ad-libbed at one point during the show, got a laugh, and that was that. I was not in another theatrical production that wasn't dance related until I was a sophomore in high school. I was cast in *The Tempest* with Tennessee Repertory Theater right before school started. TRT is a professional theater company in Nashville, and I was going to get paid for the show. The production was involved with the Humanities Outreach in Tennessee, a program at the Tennessee Performing Arts Center that sets up educational theater during the school day so students can attend performances as field trips and teachers can teach the lessons provided by HOT.

I was very excited when I got the part because my former honors English teacher had told us that the best way to learn Shakespeare was to perform it. However, I would have to miss nearly thirty days of school for rehearsals, educational performances, and question-and-answer sessions. Thankfully, my principals in elementary and junior high had always encouraged my career and never had a problem with me missing school for work since I made good grades and always completed my homework on time. But I'd had some trouble during my freshman year when I was at a new school with a new principal. I'd had to miss a few days for rehearsals at TPAC for *The Nutcracker* with Nashville Ballet. Just to be safe, my mom called my principal to make sure I would not be penalized for missing classes for educational performances. The principal said that I would get a zero for every day that I missed, regardless of what it was for. That many absences would result in my failure of my sophomore year. My parents and I thought about switching to a private school but instead decided that homeschooling would be the best option so that I could work on my own schedule and not have to deal with the restrictions of the school day.

The next year, I got a call from the director of *The Tempest* to see if I was interested in a part in *A Christmas Carol* with Tennessee Repertory Theater. I was very excited to be offered a part without the stress and the wait-and-see of auditioning. I was also lucky to have time before we started rehearsals to learn a proper British accent. We did not have cable, so I watched a lot of PBS, growing up. As a result, I fell in love with British TV shows, particularly *Are You Being Served*, so I was excited about this requirement for the part. I wouldn't be able to be in the *Nutcracker* with the Nashville Ballet like I had been for the past few years, but I would get paid for this unlike working for experience in the *Nutcracker*. I figured it would be nice to do something different for a change, and it definitely wasn't as chaotic as *Nutcracker*.

This show was different than other shows I had been in for a few reasons. We only had two weeks of rehearsals instead of three, and we were starting in the theater instead of a rehearsal space. This was the first show I performed in that was not at the Tennessee Performing Arts Center. The show was at the Acuff Theater at Opryland, right next to the Grand Ole Opry.

I played the Ghost of Christmas Past and a caroler. I shared the part with three other girls: Tyler, Kristen, and Lauren. We were like one entity, and all our lines were split up. We moved around the stage like floating spirits as we led Scrooge through his past.

*A Christmas Carol* was my favorite show. The cast was full of fun and talented actors. We spent a lot of time together, so I felt lucky to have such a good group of people to work with. I knew the director and choreographer from *The Tempest*. We had an awesome set with lots of moving pieces that entertained us between shows. Every night before the show, the crew would check the moving set pieces to make sure they worked. The front part of the stage would flip up to reveal the graveyard where the Ghost of Christmas Future took Scrooge. All the kids and whichever cast members wanted to take part would go lie down with our feet at the seam in the stage. Then the tech person would turn it on, and the stage would slowly lift and stand us up. Then it would lay us back down on the stage. We had such a fun time with that. There was also a doughnut set in the middle of the stage. The show involved three sets, the doughnut turned so that the audience could see a new set like Bob Cratchit's living room or Scrooge's office. The actors could also enter from backstage to be on the set without being seen before the set turned to the next scene.

The Ghost of Christmas Present had a little golf cart that looked like a horn of plenty that she drove around the set. I had finally received my driver's license at the end of the summer, so the crew let me drive the car. Crewmembers would run in front of me as I drove it around. I would pretend like I was driving on Broadway downtown and had to swerve to avoid hitting people.

The show had kids of all ages as cast members. The youngest two were about six, Fan and Tiny Tim, who was actually a girl. Then there was Lauren (eight), Kristen (nine), Joe (ten), Tyler (twelve), Brandon (fourteen), and myself (seventeen). Most of us were homeschooled because it worked better for our busy work schedules. Since I could drive, I helped out the Foltz family by picking their kids up during the day when we had to be at the theater during school or work hours. Whenever we could, we would always do something fun like drive to the mall and add to our Beanie Baby collections or go Christmas shopping. We had a lot of adventures.

The best part was that it was Christmas every day. *Christmas Carol* had the longest run of any play or show I had ever done. We started shows in November and went right through Christmas. We had sometimes four, two-show days a week. Opryland fed the cast between shows on the days we had two a night. We would all head over to the park next door and eat at the cafeteria there. I had to bring my own food, but we all shared a meal together at least four times a week. The cafeteria had televisions all around where they showed holiday movies. We saw the same two sections of *Rudolph the Red-Nosed Reindeer* and *It's a Wonderful Life* so many times. This was during the last few months that Opryland Theme Park was open. We could get into what was still open at the park for free, so we took advantage when we had time.

The cast had decided to do Secret Santa gifts for a week. All of the cast and crewmembers were involved except for Brooke who played Belle. The kids and I decided we did not want her to be left out, so we rotated getting gifts for her. The Foltz kids had a Winnie the Pooh cake mold. The four of us decided to make her a cake together. I went to their house during the day, and we took turns working on the cake and jumping on their trampoline in the backyard. We even decorated the cake with different icing colors using food coloring and special piping tips for the pastry bag. We bit off a little more than we could chew and ended up getting food coloring on us. The youngest also had it all over her face since she kept eating the icing. We had a performance that night we needed to be clean for, and we did not want Brooke to know that we'd made her the cake. We washed and scrubbed our hands with little result. After a while I couldn't tell if our hands were red from the washing or from the food coloring. We tried all different kinds of soap and even rubbed our hands with hydrogen peroxide. Finally, we were done, and it was time to go to the theater and try to sneak in the cake. Brooke loved it.

Along with our many roles backstage, we had multiple roles onstage. All of the past girls were also carolers except for Tyler, who also played Belinda. We all had a quick change from our caroler costumes into our ghost costumes. We had about a minute and a half to change out of our boots, dresses, caps, and cloaks into our wigs, hats, white dresses, and white boots. We also had to switch our microphone placement. It was not easy, but somehow we made it happen in every show except for one. Thank God for dress rehearsal.

Tech week came quickly, and we started to put the show together with the lights, set, and costumes. Tech week can be agonizing. We had to wait for the lights to be put in the right place, and then we often had to start a line or a scene over only to stop and wait again because the wrong light cue came up. We got to the end of the tech week, and it was time for dress rehearsal. We were all very excited to finally be in our costumes. Opening night was just around the corner.

Not all of us were prepared for the quick change. Kristen had a little trouble because it was her first experience with a quick change. We were trying to get through the show without stopping, so we had to keep going no matter what happened. Kristen had to change mics with another actor during her quick change, and that person did not get backstage fast enough. By the time that person arrived backstage and had removed her mic, the dresser that would have helped Kristen with mic placement had to move on to dress the next person. The dresser instead handed Kristen the mic and told her to put it on by herself. Kristen was only nine and was not experienced with putting on her own mic. We had to run onstage the second we were dressed, so no one noticed anything out of the ordinary until we were already onstage. I noticed at first that Kristen's hat was falling off a little bit. *Oh well, keep going,* I thought. We started to dance around Scrooge. We held hands and skipped in in a circle while taunting him. That's when Kristen's hat started to slip in front of her face. We picked up speed, dancing faster around Scrooge, and Kristen's hat slipped further in front of her face. "I can't see guys! I can't see!" she said still in her British accent. We did not expect to hear her speaking out of turn still in her British accent. I guess I have to give her credit for staying in character. We tried our hardest not to laugh, even though she was cracking us up with her comments. We kept going, regaining our composure as we fanned out from the circle one by one into a line standing behind Scrooge down the stage. It was much easier to control the laughter now that we could not see her.

I had the first line and had to step out in front of Scrooge. We couldn't see anything except for Scrooge and whichever ghost had stepped out of the line. But once in front of Scrooge, we could see all the ghosts. I stepped out in front of him and started to speak. Kristen's giant bonnet was covering half her face. Only one eye stuck out triumphantly. She peered at Scrooge from behind her hat with major attitude. Whatever control I'd had over my laughter slipped away, and a stunted giggle slipped out with my line. Each girl after me did the same when she saw her face.

Once it was time for Kristen's line, we couldn't hear her voice projected from speakers. Her microphone and its long black cord had come out of her hat and had fallen all the way below her knees. It stuck out against her pearly white dress. More laughter sputtered out of each of us. The director had had enough. "Come on girls," he begged from the audience. He just wanted us to get through the scene. It was not over soon enough. The second we were done, we ran off the stage and collapsed into a pile of giggles on the floor. But like they say, a terrible dress rehearsal means a great opening night.

After we got the giggles out, the rest of the show continued without incident. Opening night came and went without issue. The dressers knew they had to keep an eye on Kristen.

Doing a show that is a classic like *A Christmas Carol* gave me a deeper understanding of Dickens because I had an up-close-and-personal view. When I had read *Great Expectations* during my last year of regular school, I did not fully understand it. But repeating *A Christmas Carol* line by line, over and over taught me something new each time. I noticed that our costumes—with their large bonnets and big sleeves—were exaggerations of the other costumes in the show. My dress and bonnet were similar in style and shape to Scrooge's jilted and forgotten girlfriend Belle, but it was much larger than hers. I realize now, the past can become larger and exaggerated as we look back. Still, it is worth the looking.

I spent a lot of time with the Foltz kids. I liked having a new group of friends outside my usual dance friends. Since I was homeschooled and had a very busy afterschool life with regular dance, acting, and voice lessons, I did not see my friends from high school anymore.

Most of the guys I hung out with in high school were from dance or shows. I had known most of them so long they were like my brothers. Except for Brandon Foltz. In no time at all I had a crush on him. He was a good Christian boy and tall, thin, and handsome. He spoke kind of like a jock—like he was most comfortable on a basketball court. I devised a plan to get my first kiss and called all the florists in Nashville and Mount Juliet until I found a florist that had real mistletoe. I secretly hung it up in the green room before a show one day. This became a game for me, trying to get him to kiss me under the mistletoe. I don't know if the rest of the cast knew what was going on, but we all had fun with the mistletoe.

When that didn't work, I went back to the florist and bought some red roses. I snuck them into his dressing room with a card that said they were from his secret admirer. Everyone was trying to decide who the secret admirer was. Brandon's mom called the secret admirer "The Phantom Florist."

I asked my friend Mary to go for a walk with me between shows one day. We walked around what was left of Opryland in the misty rain past the Christmas carolers, bonfires, and hot chocolate stands. I wanted to get away from everyone else so we could talk. I told her I didn't know if I should tell Brandon I was The Phantom Florist or if I should just let it go. Mary is very wise and encouraged me to express my feelings but not be let down if they were not returned. I did confess to Brandon one day in the dark backstage that I was The Phantom Florist and that I liked him, but he told me the feeling was not mutual. I did my best not to cry until I was safely in the bathroom of the ladies' dressing room.

When Christmas finally arrived for real, I was kind of numb to it. The holiday had lost some of its magic after I'd lived it every day for a couple of months. I was also sad to have to say good-bye to the cast I had grown so close to at our last show on Christmas Eve.

## MARILU AND I
### *Spring 1998*

When I was seventeen, I auditioned for Ann Reinking's Broadway Theater Project. I had read a story about the summer workshop in *Dance Magazine,* and it sounded like it had been created just for me! Previously, I had gone to ballet workshops in the summer. I had been disappointed by the lack of workshops where I could dance, sing, and act all at the same place. I did not want to have to choose one discipline to study over break. When I discovered that my wish for a summer musical theater workshop had been fulfilled, I was ecstatic. The auditions were only a couple of months later. The closest one was in Fort Worth, Texas, so my mom and I made plans to travel there. I auditioned, and after a couple of weeks stalking the mailbox, my decision letter finally came. I had been accepted! Not only was I going to meet Ann Reinking and dance with her, but also both Gregory Hines and Marilu Henner—whom I had adored since I was little— were going to be there. I was beyond excited and jumped up and down with joy every time I thought about what my summer was going to be like.

I immediately got down to business and researched all of the teachers and guest artists who would be there, so I would be prepared to meet them and ask questions for the question-and-answer sessions. A few weeks later, I just happened to be at home and not out at a dance class like I normally was in the afternoons. I just happened to remember that "The Rosie O'Donnell Show" was on and decided to watch. It just so happened that Marilu Henner was a guest that day. I figured I should pay close attention to her interview. I was intrigued. She had so much energy. I didn't know how I was going to keep up with her. Then she started talking about how she didn't eat dairy anymore and why. I had been allergic to dairy for most of my life but thought that I had outgrown the allergy in junior high. The things she was saying about dairy products and how they affected her made so much sense to me. I wondered if maybe I was still allergic to dairy products. I thought that could be why I was getting sick so often. I needed more information. Marilu talked about the book she'd written about health called *Marilu Henner's Total Health Makeover*. I was very interested in the topics included in her book, but she glossed over them on the show.

The next night I happened to be up late watching David Letterman. Marilu was a guest. I watched her interview and was so inspired that I decided I would go get the book right after my Saturday morning dance classes. I read the book in a week. I couldn't put it down. It was so interesting what she had to say about eating and overall health. Everything made so much sense, and I was surprised at how much our diets and our lifestyles can affect our wellness. I understood that my way of eating—or not eating—was not helpful. No wonder I did not feel well and got sick all the time. I still wanted more information. I turned to the last page, and it said, "For more information, please visit Marilu.com." I went to the computer right away and found out she was doing a book tour. She was going to be in Nashville the very next week! I couldn't believe it. I decided it would be a good idea to meet her ahead of time, so maybe I wouldn't be so nervous when she came to Broadway Theater Project. I had no idea this choice would directly affect the rest of my life.

The day of Marilu's book signing arrived, and I was already nervous, which made me cold. I arrived a little early and went to the top level of the store. I heard someone talking in the hallway right outside of the bookstore as I was wandering around. When I turned around, I saw it was

Marilu. There she was in a beautiful white suit that contrasted with her fiery red hair and huge diamond earrings. She was talking to a small group of women seated in front of her. I thought to myself that I must have read the time wrong. I didn't know there was going to be a discussion beforehand. I stood up against the wall, listening but trying not to intrude on the small group. I was clutching her book hard against my chest.

I will never forget this moment. I was standing and listening to her talk, and she stopped looking at the women. She stared at me as if I were the only person there. I couldn't figure out why she was staring at me, so I started scanning the room to see if she was looking at anyone else. There was no mistaking it; she was smiling at me, staring directly into my eyes and simultaneously scaring the crap out of me. A few minutes later, a bookstore employee came over and said, "This is for the radio winners only. You have to go downstairs for the book signing; it will start later." I was beet red. I apologized quietly to the employee and made my way downstairs.

I was even more nervous standing in line. I was still freezing, and my hands were all sweaty but ice cold. I realized I had to tell Marilu what a difference her book had already made for me. I also had to tell her that I would be at Broadway Theater Project and was looking forward to working with her. My heart was beating out of my chest. I didn't know how I was going to even say my name. Growing up, I had watched *Evening Shade,* and she was my favorite thing about it. She was so funny and had an energy that made her stand out from the rest of the cast. I had seen *Taxi* a few times and loved her in that show, as well. She made her way down the stairs and started to sign books and talk to people. As I moved closer to her table, I was short of breath. I couldn't believe how scared I was, but the excitement of meeting one of my favorite celebrities—someone whose book had helped me with my eating disorder—was just too much.

It was finally my turn. I gave her my book and said, "Hello."

She said, "Oh, I remember you from upstairs."

I was startled, but I got right to it. "I grew up watching you on *Evening Shade*," I said. "You were my favorite part of that show."

She smiled. "Thank you!" Then she looked down to sign my book.

I did not want the conversation to be over yet, but I was still very nervous about what I wanted to tell her. So I asked her a neutral question. "Are you still going to Ann Reinking's Broadway Theater Project?"

"I am in about three months."

"I am too! I am so excited about it. I can't wait to meet Ann Reinking and learn some more Fosse choreography. We did *All That Jazz* for the audition."

"Oh, you did? Was it hard to learn quickly?"

"I already knew it, so it wasn't too hard, but it was nice to learn some of the intricacies I had not realized."

I knew I needed to move along, but I really wanted to tell her how much her book meant to me. I could sense that people were listening to our conversation. I didn't know how I was going to say what I needed to say without them hearing. I took a deep breath. "Thank you so much for this book! It has totally changed my life, and I've only had it a week. It's already given me a more positive attitude about my body because I'm a dancer. I realized that it's about the quality of the food you eat and not the quantity that matters. As a dancer, thin is never thin enough—if you know what I mean."

She stopped writing and looked right into my eyes. "Oh," she said. She put her very warm hand on my very cold arm. "Well, thank you for the compliment."

I said thanks again and that I would see her that summer. I decided I needed to talk to her a little more when there weren't quite so many people around, so I went back up to the top level to read while people made their way through the book-signing line. After twenty minutes, I looked down to the bottom floor, but she was gone. My heart sank, and I figured I would just talk to her at BTP.

The next few months dragged by until finally it was July, and Broadway Theater Project was in full swing. It was so amazing. I absolutely loved it. The work was hard and the hours were long, but I was having the time of my life. Marilu was there for a day during the second week. We had a Q&A with her first. I was sitting in the front row of the audience. She was telling us stories about her life and how she got started in the entertainment business. Then she started telling us about her book tour. At one point, she told a story about meeting a young dancer at a bookstore recently. The more she talked the more it sounded like when she had met me. She even described what the young woman had said to her about her book. I always taped Q&As, and I must have listened to that story a million times, trying to figure out if she was referring to me or not.

After the Q&A, we danced the "Hot Honey Rag" from *Chicago* with her. She had been in the show on Broadway the year before. I was so excited to have the opportunity to dance with her even though it would be with all the other students, too. I was in the front row as close as I could get to where she was dancing. Usually after Q&As with guest artists, we would take pictures with them. My turn to get a picture with Marilu finally came, and I wanted to tell her how much better I was doing with my eating. I had started a food journal and had found some support for the eating disorder. It wasn't always easy, but I was on the right track. Theater kids, who were also waiting to get their pictures, surrounded me. I really wanted to talk to her, but I did not want everyone else to hear what I was saying.

I went up to get my picture, and she said through her smile as the shutter snapped, "Didn't we meet?"

I was so surprised that she even halfway remembered me! "Yes," I said. "We met in Nashville. I'm Heather, the dancer."

She said it was great to see me again and that I looked so much better. I couldn't believe she remembered me enough to make a comparison. I had often felt invisible in my life, especially during that time. The fact that she saw me and remembered me made a big impact. I felt a little caught off guard. I decided I would try to talk to her afterward and went to pack up my stuff while she finished with pictures. I waited until most everyone was gone to make my approach, but the pushy PR person started to whisk her away. Marilu was watching me as she left. I opened my mouth to say something and quickly closed it. What was the use? She looked at me like she understood. I figured I'd never see her again.

The next spring, I was getting ready to go to Broadway Theater Project again. Marilu was scheduled to be there, so I decided I should look her up again. She had a new book coming out, and I thought I might have a better opportunity to talk to her again on her book tour. I checked her schedule and was disappointed that she did not have a stop in Nashville. I would just have to wait. I decided I would get the book after my dance classes were over that afternoon.

I was so excited about this new book. I had seen her promoting it on "The Rosie O'Donnell Show," and I knew it would be very helpful to me in my health journey. I bought the book and was stuck in traffic on the way home. All I wanted to do was start reading it. I finally got home and immediately ran to the couch. I didn't take off my purse; I didn't put away my keys. I sat down, opened the book, and began to read. I normally do not read introductions to books because I just want to get to the fun part, but I wanted to read every word Marilu had written. She had begun by writing about her experience with the book tour and all the people who were excited about her ideas about eating. Then she'd written about a ballerina whom she had met in Nashville. I wondered whom she was talking about because I didn't think there was anyone else there from Nashville Ballet but me. I read on, and she said she'd met this same dancer a few months later at Ann Reinking's Broadway Theater Project.

Now I was really confused! I knew for sure I was the only person at BTP from Nashville—if not from all of Tennessee! I couldn't figure out whom she was talking about, and she didn't use a name, which did not help. The more I read, the more familiar the story seemed. It had to be me. I started saying, "Oh my God," over and over at an increasing volume until my brother, who was in the kitchen, asked what was wrong. "Ummmm nothing," I said.

I went to my room to think. I needed to figure this out. It couldn't be me. There was no way my favorite actress (outside of Barbra Streisand) and a *New York Times* bestselling author had written about me in her book. No way. I needed outside opinions. I'd never told any of my friends about my eating disorder, which she mentioned in the passage, but I would have to get over that because I needed to know what they thought. I called my best friend at the time and read the paragraph to her.

"It's you," she said.

"Are you sure?" I asked.

"Yes. It has to be you."

"I don't understand it. Why would she write about me?"

"I don't know why, but I know it's you."

I called another friend and read it to her. Once again she said it was me. She was really excited about it and thought it was pretty cool. I still did not believe it. The next day I told the ballet teacher I was closest to. She said, "See, Heather! You do make an impact on people." I still didn't believe it. I needed confirmation from the source.

July came around, and I was at Broadway Theater Project again. Not long before Marilu was supposed to come, we found out she wasn't available to be there that summer because she was playing Roxie Hart in *Chicago* in Las Vegas. Her husband at the time, Director Rob Liberman, would be there instead. I was upset that I wasn't going to get confirmation from her that she'd written about me in the introduction of her new book. It was driving me crazy, and there was a very good chance I would never find out. Rob turned out to be great, and I learned a lot from his Q&A session. I met him afterward and got a picture with him. I don't know what possessed me, but I told him I was not very happy with Marilu for not coming. I needed to ask her a very important question about her book, and I hoped he would tell her that. He was around the next day with apologies from Marilu. I couldn't believe it.

That August I moved to New York City for college. It turned out Marilu had a new book out and would be in the city for a book signing in October. I was so excited. Finally, I would get an answer.

The day of the book signing arrived, and I went uptown to the Barnes and Noble on the Upper East Side. Marilu held a discussion about the book first. She saw me in the audience while they were introducing her, and she waved to me. I was once again surprised that she had remembered me. During the book discussion, she said she was going to start hosting health classes on her website to help people implement the lifestyle changes she wrote about. I thought this was genius. She said she'd be asking people if they wanted to teach a class. I wanted her to ask me. I really wanted to teach a class! But I knew she wouldn't ask me since I was only eighteen and a freshman in college.

After the discussion, she signed books. When it was my turn, she said she was so sorry she could not make it to BTP the summer before and that Rob had told her I was mad she wasn't there! I couldn't believe she remembered. I apologized and turned red. I grabbed the book in question and opened it to the introduction. I glanced around and leaned in so people wouldn't hear me. "Well, I wanted to talk to you at BTP because I needed to know if this was me." I pointed to the part in the introduction she had written about the dancer from Nashville.

She looked at the book and kind of whispered back, "Yes, that's you."

I was surprised but happy to at last have confirmation.

Marilu started classes on her website that spring like she

had discussed, and I joined in. I learned so much about myself and food and how to turn her ideas about food into a lifestyle. It took some time to make all those changes, but by the spring of sophomore year I started to see and feel a difference. I loved how I felt when I ate more "clean" food and didn't eat dairy and refined sugar. I started to lose the weight I had gained since starting college. I exercised and enjoyed it. I would go to bed at midnight, and my eyes would pop open at six. I felt fully awake then and ready to start the day. After spending my freshman year with a giant Starbucks cup permanently glued to my hand, I didn't need coffee anymore by the end of sophomore year. I had plenty of natural energy. My life was great.

Marilu had hosted a spa weekend with some of the people from her website the year before and decided to do it again in the spring of 2001. I had saved so much money from eating healthy and not drinking coffee that I was able to attend. I had not been on a vacation by myself. My only solo travels were flights between New York and Nashville. I had never traveled farther west than Little Rock, let alone across the country. But I decided I was going to go.

It turned out that the dates for the spa weekend were right in the middle of finals, but I would not be deterred. I figured that counting flight time and airport connections time, I'd have twelve hours during my travel to study. If I was in New York, I'd be packing up my stuff for the summer rather than studying the whole time anyway. My grades were great, and I was going to the spa no matter what.

I met up with a friend at LAX, and we drove to Palm Springs for the spa weekend. I couldn't get over the miles of windmills. They were so beautiful, all white and uniform. The desert was so interesting to me. I found the lack of trees and the visible sharp edges of the mountains jarring but also stunning. It was so different than the rolling, tree-covered hills I had grown up with in Tennessee. There were palm trees everywhere, and it was so warm. I loved it already.

I was looking forward to seeing Marilu again and to

meeting my new friends from the online classes. I had learned the choreography from a few numbers from *Chicago* and had asked Marilu if we could do the "Hot Honey Rag" together at the spa. She said yes, and I was elated. I was going to dance with Marilu—just the two of us!

That Saturday after dinner, we all gathered in the exercise room for fun and karaoke. Marilu and I did the "Hot Honey Rag" together, and it was so much fun. I worked so hard to make sure every single little move was executed correctly, and it meant the world to me that she could see that. She believed in me as a dancer. I wasn't used to that, people believing in me. She was very complimentary of my dancing, and I was quite surprised. It was only the beginning of what has become a beautiful friendship.

I have had a lot of strange health problems because of my allergies and Lyme Disease. When I was really sick from the Lyme but did not have a diagnosis yet, Marilu tried to help me figure out what was wrong. She suggested remedies to help me with the symptoms while I was in search of a diagnosis. Once I found a diagnosis, she helped me navigate some of the difficulties in living with Lyme. I did finally become a health coach for her website. I love teaching classes and empowering people to become healthier—just like she helped me on my journey toward wellness.

## PEOPLE WHO NEED BARBRA
*Fall 1993*

I love Barbra Streisand. So much of my life is connected to hers in weird little ways no one could ever understand, and I won't bother to explain. Barbra filled me up when the world cut me down. She introduced me to musicals, Broadway, love, and New York City— places that I would soon go and that would change my life. I have been a fan of hers since I was twelve. What a year that was. I still remember the first time I heard her sing. It was September of 1993. A friend had brought her *Back to Broadway* tape for me to listen to for songs for the upcoming year of pageant talent competitions. When I heard her sing the first song on the tape, "Some Enchanted Evening," something inside of me turned on—a part of me that had always been there but I had never known was coming to the surface.

I had so many questions once the song was finished. *Who is this? What type of song is she singing? How long has she been around? Does she have any other albums?* At this point in time, I did not really know what Broadway was. She was my introduction to the profession I have found myself working towards or longing for most of my life. I just knew there was more to the songs she sang on that album. The liner notes did not have much information about the shows that the songs were from, so I decided to find out more about them for myself. I was fascinated with the larger stories that the songs told. I loved the idea of telling a story through music and watching it all unfold live right in front of me or being a part of the storytelling on stage.

My friend gave me the tape, and I listened to it so much that it became so worn and stretched it didn't sound like Barbra anymore. I would listen to it in the car, when I couldn't sleep, and when I just wanted to sing. My mother and I must have listened to "Everybody Says Don't" a hundred times, trying to figure out the lyrics. I loved it so much and was planning to sing it for the state pageant. She sang so fast we would get so excited when we figured out a word in a line.

I kept the tape, even though it was damaged, and I still have it, because it was so soothing and reassuring to me. Adolescence was a tempestuous time in my life, and her voice was my sanctuary. It was my reassurance that there was somewhere to go, and I was going there.

The tape now sits in the very center of the memory box a friend made for me when I was eighteen. The tape is a representation of that moment in my life when everything around me started to change and become something different. It is the only concrete thing I have that marks the end of my childhood and the start of my adult life in so many ways. It is like the badge on a Girl Scout's sash, designating that she sold a thousand boxes of cookies. I imagine that Barbra Streisand could never know what a little lump of plastic and magnetic tape with her name and voice attached could represent to a twelve-year-old girl.

I remember glances of Barbra in my life before I knew who she was or what she did. Whenever my brother and I were allowed to pick out a tape to rent at the grocery store in our neighborhood, I would see *Funny Girl* and wonder what it was. I would look at the red and white box with the illustration of the upside down girl in roller-skates—with the title of the movie standing in for her dress. I was intrigued by this movie, but I never rented it. I guess it was too soon. I was not ready for the avalanche of emotions and awe that would be my first viewing of *Funny Girl*.

A few years later, I just happened to see an old Siskel and

Ebert review of *Yentl*. They showed clips of the film, and I was intrigued. I did not know why, but I felt I had to see that movie. I was drawn to it. The plot was different than any other movie I had seen, and the actress was just so striking in her beauty and talent. I did not know it was Barbra Streisand. I was not quite old enough to see it yet. I forgot the title but the images and the story stuck with me.

After I finally knew who Barbra was, my mom said I needed to see *Funny Girl*. We bought the videotape along with *The Way We Were*. I locked myself in my parents' bedroom by myself to watch *Funny Girl* for the first time. I did not know what it was about, but I put the tape in and sat on the bed to find out. I was a little confused since the movie started at the end of the story. Despite my confusion, I was captivated from the time she appeared on screen until the end of her big showstopper, "I'm the Greatest Star." I sat at the edge of the bed blown away by the song, her voice, and her diverse acting skills. I wanted more. The rest of the movie did not disappoint. I was hooked on this funny lady and pledged my allegiance right then and there with my Barbie dolls as my witness.

Barbra's work is such a part of who I am. Her music has shaped my life in a way nothing else has. Growing up, I spent a lot of time trying to imitate her tone and the way she sings specific songs. In some ways, listening to her taught me how to sing. I learned the importance of using my voice to convey emotion because her singing had such a profound effect on my own emotions. I have wondered about the pain she may have gone through to get so in touch with her feelings. It sometimes sounds as if her vocal chords are connected to her heartstrings. In my opinion, Billie Holiday is the only singer whose passion rivals that of Barbra.

As I collected her albums, I gave them each a purpose in my life. *A Happening in Central Park* was music to clean to. I loved singing along and imitating her delivery. One day in New York, I was cleaning my room and singing at the top of my lungs, doing my best Barbra imitation. I thought I was alone. I later found out my roommate's boyfriend was in the other room. He'd told her he was very impressed with my singing skills.

*Back to Broadway* became my thinking music. If I had a problem, I would listen to that album, and the familiarity of the music would help me make a choice. As an Aries, I can often become overly excited. Once I found *Simply Streisand*, it became my calm-down-and-relax music. My early twenties were a time of growth and change that involved a lot of nervous energy. If something put butterflies in my stomach, all I had to do was listen to *Simply Streisand*, and remember to breathe. The butterflies flew away with each note she sang.

If I was in love, I listened to *The Barbra Streisand Album*. I would sing and dance to "Keepin' Out of Mischief Now" and "My Honey's Lovin' Arms." I would imagine the guy I had a crush on as I sang, and my heart was just as full as Barbra's when she was singing. When a love interest did not appear to return my feelings, I would sing all the sorrow and pain out with "Cry Me a River."

*A Love Like Ours* was released when I was a freshman in college. It was on rotation along with Ani DiFranco and Ben Folds Five on my roommate's stereo. Three of us who lived together would listen to it while studying at night. That album reminds me of watching the sun set over Brooklyn back when New York was still new and exciting to me.

The many times I have tried to learn to speak French, I have listened to her French album *Je m'appelle Barbra*. I can explain what "Clopin-Clopant" means, but please don't ask me to figure out how to construct a sentence in French that is not in one of the songs.

I love Christmas music, and my favorite song is "Have Yourself a Merry Little Christmas." I still remember the first time I heard her version at a jewelry store when I was twelve. I was very surprised that she made a Christmas album, but I got my own copy right away and still listen to it every year.

In college I worked at Lincoln Center Theater for a while as a bartender. There was a Tower Records a couple blocks away. I used to go there on Saturdays between shows and flip through the giant section of Barbra CDs. They were having a sale on her albums for a few months. I figured out that the price tags had a spot on them that said how long an album would be on sale. They were not on sale all at once, which is a good thing because there were about forty that I did not have yet. I would spend my tip money on her albums, spacing them out with the goal of completing my collection. I was so excited to rip open the plastic and put the new disc in my Walkman to listen to it on the subway on my way back to Brooklyn. Her music became like a good friend I could always count on to get me through the tough times in life and cheer me on through the happy times. I needed Barbra and her music. I have rarely encountered a person who knew me well who dared to touch my heart so deeply.

I remember listening to *Barbra: The Concert CD* the summer of 1994. I would lie on my bed and dream about the day that I would see her live in concert at Madison Square Garden. It had to happen someday. I begged my parents to let me go to Vegas and see her in concert on New Year's Eve. I wondered why she couldn't come to Nashville on her tour. At that time, I had no idea of the magnitude of her career. Barbra only had to do a few concerts whenever she felt like it. She didn't have to travel all over because people would travel to see her.

I would sing along to "Evergreen" while listening to her concert CD and wonder what she was doing while I was listening. When I was sixteen, I bought my first book about Barbra by James Spader. I read that she had tinnitus. I had no idea that a constant ringing in your ears was not normal. It had been something that had bothered me for years. The quieter it got in the house, the louder it became in my ears. I had never complained about it because I thought it was just the way it was. I would listen to Barbra and sing along as a way to overcome the annoying buzzing in my ears.

When I got to college in 1999 and had to write papers, I found that there were a few albums that helped me write.

One of the three was *Barbra Streisand The Concert Disc 2*. I am listening to it right now. If I can't find the right words when I am writing, all I have to do is press play, and there they are on the page like magic.

In the summer of 2000, I heard a rumor at Ann Reinking's Broadway Theater Project that Barbra was having a concert. I thought it was a cruel joke and didn't think about it again until that fall when I returned to New York and found out it was true. I was broke from not working that summer, and the only tickets left were $1,000 minimum. I did everything I could think of to try and get a ticket. I called Madison Square Garden and left a message, saying I was writing a story about it for my college paper. I asked all the people I worked with at Lincoln Center Theater that might have connections for a ticket. I had no luck. I was so depressed. I was finally in the same city where she was performing, but I couldn't afford to attend.

I bought the *Timeless Concert CD* from the concert tour I'd missed the day it came out. I listened to it a few times, but I have a hard time listening to it. It just makes me cry. Ever since I'd heard Barbra's duet of "The Music of the Night" with Michael Crawford, my ultimate goal in life has been to sing a duet with her. If I do that, I can die. There was a young girl who not only got to meet Barbra but also sang some duets with her in the *Timeless* concert. I hated her because I wanted it to be me. I wanted so badly to be the young Barbra and sing with the real Barbra in concert. I could do a pretty good imitation of her. I looked young enough. I could wear a prosthetic nose if needed. I could have a Brooklyn accent. I lived in Brooklyn! But it was not meant to be. I still hold onto hope that one day it will finally happen—even if it's just a few lines of a song.

My love for Barbra is a part of my personality that those whom I know and love have come to understand and, at the very least, tolerate. People often tease me and call me a gay man for loving her so much, but I don't know how to not love her. I guess I'm just a person who needs Barbra.

# ACKNOWLEDGEMENTS

I have a lot of people to thank who helped me on the long journey of writing this book. Thank you to everyone who bought my chapbook and wanted more. Your comments and encouragement kept me going. Thank you, Renee, for being my first reader and cheerleader. Thank you, Jane Wells, for publishing me for the first time on CNBC.com and also for listening to my stories and telling me to write them down. Thank you, Victoria Ladd, for telling me to write a book in the first place. I was just waiting for someone to tell me to do it. Thank you to my friends for saying yes to adventure. Thank you, Marilu, for believing in me and letting me be a part of your team. Thank you for helping me to figure out my health issues. If it wasn't for you I probably would not be here today.

I am so grateful to Lisa Binder for introducing me to Merrill Farnsworth and telling me to do what I love. I was lucky to have Merrill Farnsworth and her Writing Circles to get writing done and receive feedback quickly. Thank you to all of my circle members especially Missy, Gabrielle, Julie, Mary Elle, Kyndyll, Tobi, Jessica, Jamie, Rain, and Tammy.

Thank you to my awesome editor, Jennifer Chesak. You have helped me to become a better writer. I so appreciate you taking a chance on me. Thank you to my parents for letting me lead an interesting life. Without your encouragement and support, I would not have had the courage to do any of these things. Thank you so much to my husband, Steven. You are there to lift me up when I think I can't do it anymore. I am so glad we finally found each other. My life would suck without you.

# ABOUT THE AUTHOR

Heather Holloway has been writing and telling stories since she was a little girl. She has worked in various fields including entertainment, Wall Street, and fitness, starting at age eight. She has had featured writing published on CNBC.com. Also, SaveTheAssistants.com and Ronebreak.com have published her work. She made the best of Craigslist New York in 2009. She read at Howlin' Books for Howlin' After Dark where her chapbook, *Making Shit Up in My Head*, sold out in 2014. Her blog is HeatherHollowayMcCash.com. In addition to writing, she is a Pilates, Xtend Barre, and TRX Instructor. Heather lives in Nashville with her husband, Steven, and hopes to meet Barbra Streisand one day.